SHROPSHIRE COUNTY LIBRARY SERVICE

www.shropshireonline.gov.uk/library.nsf

Please return or renew before the last date
stamped below. You can renew by person, by
telephone or on the web site, unless it Is
required by another user.

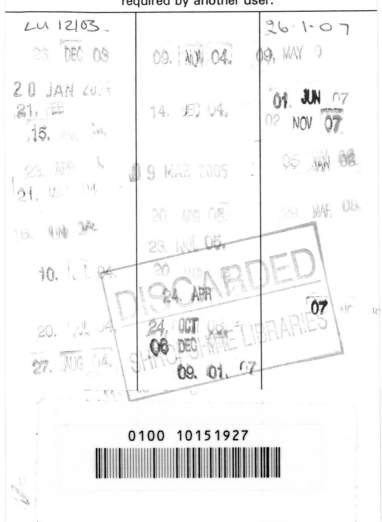

Everyday Spells for a Teenage Witch

Marie Bruce

quantum
LONDON • NEW YORK • TORONTO • SYDNEY

quantum

An imprint of W. Foulsham & Co. Ltd
The Publishing House, Bennetts Close, Cippenham,
Slough, Berkshire, SL1 5AP, England

ISBN 0-572-02770-2

Copyright © 2002 W. Foulsham and Co. Ltd

Cover illustration by Jurgen Ziewe

Printed in Great Britain by St Edmundsbury Press, Bury St Edmunds, Suffolk

Contents

So ...
You Want
to Be
Sabrina?

If you've ever had a really bad hair day ... if you've ever sat hugging your mobile phone waiting for him to call ... if you've ever agonised over science tests and exams ... then worry no more – this is the book for you.

If you've picked up this book then you are obviously interested in witchcraft. Maybe your interest began after seeing a film or TV series such as *Charmed*, *Practical Magic*, *The Craft*, or *Sabrina, the Teenage Witch*. Maybe you've developed an interest in Wicca and would like to learn more. Or perhaps you picked up this book simply out of curiosity.

The truth is that how you came to be reading these words isn't really important. My guess is you're reading them because you want to learn how to cast spells, perform rituals and work magic to put the wrong things right. My guess is that deep down, you are already a witch!

If you want to cast hexes and curse people, then you picked the wrong witch as your tutor. I am a good witch and this is a book of white magic. You will find no dark arts within these pages. What you will find are spells to help with homework, make a boy notice you, stop parents hassling you, deal with bullies and gossips, release anger and increase your pocket money. Add to this weather witching and faerie magic; love spells, money spells and protection spells; a chapter of lotions and potions; and information about the traditional witches' sabbats ... and what you have is a practical handbook for the practice of witchcraft.

Everyday Spells for a Teenage Witch is written just for you, with your problems and your needs in mind. A book that has been designed and created especially for the teenage girls of today – the women and witches of tomorrow. So turn off the TV and come and cast some spells with me.

Happy casting!

Morgana

All About Witchcraft

This book will teach you how to lead a charmed life. What you hold in your hands right now is a magical text book, a tool of power and the key to taking control of your destiny.

Witchcraft works. It works for me every day and it can work for you too. For me, the best thing about being a witch is that I am in control of my life, and any problems can be resolved with a little magic. And if anyone could use a little magic in their lives, it's teenagers.

Being a teenager is tough because you have so many things to deal with. Your body is going through major changes, your hormones are everywhere, your mind is trying to move forwards into adulthood, and, to top it all, the Department of Education dictates that now is the time for you to sit some of the most important examinations of your life – like you don't have enough to think about!

You are constantly in the middle of a crush or a crisis, a spot the size of Mount Etna has erupted on your face and you're convinced you're adopted – either that or your parents are from another planet.

When I was young, I found that one of the most annoying things adults could do was give me the 'best years of your life' speech. You know, the one where they tell you how great your life is, how you have no responsibilities, no problems and nothing at all to worry about. These are people who have forgotten what it's like to be young.

Now, at the ripe old age of 27 (yes, I'm that old!), I can sort of understand what they meant. At 14 I had no mortgage or rent, no bills, no family commitments and so on. But I had worries of my own – like crying buckets over my algebra homework and quaking at the knees at the thought of my

French oral exam. Not to mention the fact that I seemed to be a complete dork magnet. None of the trendy lads gave me a second glance – but every geek with a Transformer came knocking on my door.

These were the kind of problems I had. Probably not a million miles away from the kind of problems you have yourself. Young people do have responsibilities and they do have worries. So if it matters to you, then it matters. Let no one tell you otherwise.

There are all sorts of spells in this book that will help you to iron out life's little wrinkles. But before you go flicking through the pages trying to get to the 'good bit', there are a few things you need to know before you can cast an effective spell. So read on ...

the truth about white magic

Magic can and will change your life for the better providing you are sensible and use it correctly and responsibly. Being a witch means taking full responsibility for your actions and following the rules. Yes, Wicca has rules too, but not many.

The first rule of white magic is that all spells should be cast with harm to none. This is known as the Wiccan Rede and it goes like this:

◎ *If it **harms none**, do what you will.*

In this instance harm none includes yourself and the animal kingdom. So before you cast a spell, you must think very carefully about just who your magic will affect and how it will affect them, as witches believe that whatever we send out we get back times three. A very good reason to keep your witchcraft white.

At the end of each spell I cast, I follow up with the words:

◎ *I cast this spell with **harm to none**, or I declare this spell **undone**.*

This statement ensures that my spell will harm no one. Or if it is likely to cause harm in a way I have overlooked, then this final sentence will make the spell powerless and the magic won't work.

Although all the spells in this book follow the Wiccan Rede and harm none, I suggest that you get into the habit of adding the above sentence to all the spells you cast. Then, by the time you are ready to create your own spells, it will have become second nature and none of your magic will backfire on you.

Another Wiccan no-no is using magic to make a person do what you want. This is known as 'bending will' and is a purely selfish act. Good witches don't mess around with another person's free will. We cast our spells around ourselves, not directly on another person. Spells that work to bend someone's will come under the category of dark magic. True witches don't play with that particular wand as it has a tendency to bite you on the bum!

So long as you keep your magic pure, in accordance with the Wiccan Rede, and you cast your spells only around yourself (unless you have permission to work a healing ritual for someone), then your spells will be powerful, effective and life-improving.

how magic works

Magic works by like attracting like. What you focus on is what you get, and witches know the power of positive thinking. Thoughts have power and they are the first step of magic. In order for any spell to work you must first think of the desired outcome – we call this the magical goal. By imagining what you want as if it has already happened you are sowing the seeds of magic.

For example, as a child Madonna spent many hours day-dreaming about being a famous singer and dancer. She knew that she wanted to sing, dance, be famous and make people happy through her work. She imagined her goal, focused on it and worked very hard to bring it into being. And what do you know? – her dream came true!

Focus and willpower are the backbone of any magical casting. Don't think of the obstacles or barriers that block the way to your goal. Think only of achieving that goal and you will be setting yourself up for success.

As a young person, you have time on your side and you can be whatever you want to be. All you have to do is focus, remain positive and work hard at what you truly want to do. Add a dash of magic and you are well on your way to success.

Witches use a variety of tools such as candles, herbs, oils, and so on as a representation of their magical need. In order for magic to work you must not only want but also *need* what you are spelling for (this is a Wiccan term – witches 'spell' or 'cast' for what we desire). That means that if you have four chocolate bars in the house and you cast for another one, you are unlikely to get it as you are already well provided for in the chocolate department. But maybe you need some peace and quiet so that you can do your homework or study for an exam. This is a genuine need and such a spell will be effective. Preventative spells are also effective. These are the spells you cast on a daily basis to protect your home or your bike or to keep you safe on your walk to and from school. You will find all such spells in this book.

where does magic come from?

Magic comes from two sources – inside and outside. It's that easy. Magic comes from inside because we all hold a spark of magic inside us. We just have to bring that spark to the surface. This is where nifty props can help. By using tools such as a wand and a pentacle, or by lighting candles and incense you are connecting with your inner magic and putting yourself in a witchy mood. This makes you feel magical, and when you feel magical you know that you are ready to zap!

Magic also comes from outside, or from the natural world around us. In this sense magic can be found in trees, flowers, rocks, streams, rain and so on. This type of magic is known as the universal power. Witches use objects of nature, such as feathers, pebbles, sea-shells and so on, to connect with this power.

For a spell to work, the witch has to weave her own inner magic with the magic of the universe. There are several ways to do this, for example by burning or burying a spell. We will explore these ways in the spells of this book.

how spells manifest

When a spell works, witches call this manifestation. This means that a spell has moved our desire from the magical world into the physical one. In other words, the spell we cast to pass an exam manifests as a C grade or above.

Magic always works in the easiest way, or by 'the path of least resistance'. This means that when a spell has worked it can often look like coincidence. But to witches there really is no such thing as coincidence. We believe that everything happens for a reason – even the bad things have something to teach us. So when you cast a spell, don't put it down to coincidence when it works. Give yourself a pat on the back and be confident in your witchy powers.

How long a spell takes to work depends entirely on the type of spell cast. A small spell, one to increase pocket money for instance, will usually manifest more quickly than a spell for a new bike or a family holiday. As a general rule, small spells take around one lunar month (from full moon to full moon) to manifest, while larger spells can take up to six months and sometimes longer.

I'll give you an example of a relatively large spell. On New Year's Day 2001, I cast a candle spell to gain a second book contract with my publishers. (For more information on candle magic see my book *Candleburning Rituals*.) On 2 February – Imbolc, no less, a witches' sabbat or festival – I received a letter asking if I was interested in writing a book on witchcraft aimed at teenagers. Was I?! At the beginning of April I signed the publishing contract for *Everyday Spells for a Teenage Witch*. The whole process took four months, from casting the spell to signing the contract and beginning to write the book. Now four months may seem like a long time, but this was quite a large spell remember, as there are many people along the way who have to be persuaded that a book is worth publishing. And it does illustrate my main point – witchcraft works. Yes, it can take a little time and, yes, it can often appear to be coincidental, but the simple truth is, magic works and witchcraft gets results. Now wouldn't you just love to have that power for yourself? By the end of this book, you will have.

support your spells

Every spell you cast must be supported in the everyday world. This means that if you cast a spell to lose weight, you should exercise and eat healthily. This is known as backing up your magic. All the diet spells in the world won't work if you stuff yourself with crisps and chip butties every day. If you are doing everything you can to achieve your goal in the mundane world then your spell will manifest – because you are giving it no choice. So even though you have zapped your brains out casting 'success in exams' spells, you still have to revise and study. I know, it's a bummer! But witchcraft works best for those who help themselves.

deciding to become a witch

Okay, so you've read all the rules; you know how magic works, where the power comes from and how spells manifest. You know you have to back up all your spells and cast them with harm to none. What next?

Well, now you have to decide to become a witch. This means taking full responsibility for all your thoughts, words and actions. It means practising witchcraft to make your life run smoothly – or as smoothly as anyone's life can run. We all come across bumps in the road now and then, but as a witch you can use your magic to help you over these bumps and then move swiftly on.

There are many wannabes out there. Life is full of wannabe actors, wannabe pop-stars and wannabe models. There is nothing wrong with this – we all have to start somewhere and, as I said earlier, a dream is a valuable goal to aim for and turn into a reality. The danger lies in being content to be a wannabe. You have to focus on your dream and work really hard to make it happen. There is no such thing as an 'overnight success'. Behind every success story lies a tale of courage, hard work, determination and probably tears. I know. I was a wannabe writer for years before I finally had my first book published. And, yes, magic and witchcraft did help me to achieve my dream. My advice to you is, never give up on your dream – you may give up on the very day that success was due to knock on your door.

And whatever you do, don't become a wannabe witch! There are people around who drape themselves in black, drip with pentagram jewellery, call themselves a witch and yet have never cast a spell. Others barely move beyond a simple altar set-up and reading about Wicca. Don't go down that road. You can't call yourself a witch unless you work rituals, observe the sabbats and cast spells. So don't be a wannabe witch – be a witch, and use the magic of the Craft to help you reach your other wannabe goals.

choosing a magical name

Most witches have a magical name. It helps us to connect with our witchy selves and leave the ordinary world behind for a while. Some witches keep their magical name to themselves and treat it as a secret, while others declare their name to the world. I have three magical names, two of which are secret and are known only to the universe and myself. My third magical name is Morgana, and I often use this name in my writing or when signing Craft letters to friends.

Your first task then is to choose your own magical name. This can be the name of a Goddess of mythology such as Rhiannon, Diana, Artemis and so on. Or you might decide to look to nature and come up with Birdsong, Cloud, Autumn, Rainbow, etc. Let your imagination run wild. This is a name that you (not your parents) get to choose, so make it special. Make it magical. Once you have chosen your new name, you are ready to perform your first ritual!

craft dedication ritual

Whenever you perform a spell or a ritual, it will have a specific purpose for you to concentrate on (what you want), there will be a few things you need, and there will usually be an ideal time in the moon's cycle to perform the ritual (moon time). I've listed all this information for this first ritual, but I'll explain all about it later.

> **What you want:** *to declare yourself a Witch.*
> **What you need:** *a white candle and holder, an inscribing tool (a knitting needle will do), a piece of paper with your magical name written on it, an ashtray, matches.*
> **Moon time:** *new or full.*

◎ **Have a nice relaxing bath and wash away the stresses of the day.**

- Go to a quiet place on the night of your chosen moon phase; this can be indoors or outdoors.

- With the inscribing tool, write your new magical name on the white candle. Set it firmly in the holder and then light it.

- Now concentrate on the flame and hold the paper with your new name written on it. Chant the name softly to yourself until it feels natural, until it feels as if this name fits you. At that point your state of mind has changed and you have moved from the everyday person to the witch. Get to know this feeling, as this is the state of mind you need to cast spells.

- After a few minutes, burn the paper in the candle flame and drop it in the ashtray – be very careful! Now blow out the candle and keep it in a safe place.

This candle now represents your new witchy powers, and you can light it and make power wishes on it whenever you have a small need, before blowing out the flame. (For safety's sake, remember never to leave a candle burning unattended.)

Tools of the Craft

Before we begin spell-casting, let's go through all that a witch needs to make her magic happen. Some books will tell you that you need lots of expensive tools in order for your spells to work. Rubbish! I find that some of the most powerful tools I use are the ones found in nature. Yes, it's nice to have two or three attractive packs of tarot cards, a beautiful crystal ball, a pendulum, rune stones and a pewter chalice, but none of these things is essential. Remember that *you*, not your tools, are the magic.

For the spells and rituals in this book you will need a pentacle, a wand, a chalice and some sort of cauldron, but you can easily make these tools at home, so they need not cost a vast amount of money. We will also be casting some nifty spells with things that you can find lying around the house, such as ribbons and thread, paints, nail polish, balloons and make-up, plus we'll be using simple tools such as dried herbs, candles and tea-lights, crayons, crystals, oils and oil burners and so on. After a number of years in the Craft, I have collected several beautiful magical tools, but that has taken time, and many of them cost nothing as I either made them or found them.

But so that you know the basics before you start casting spells, let's take a look at some of the standard tools witches use.

the pentacle

The pentacle is a disc with a five-pointed star inscribed upon it. This star is known as a pentagram. Pentacles are usually made of wood, clay or slate. As a tool, the pentacle is used to charge other tools, talismans, herbs and so on with magical power. This is done by placing the object in the centre of the star. The pentacle can also be used in protection and is invaluable in prosperity spells.

The pentacle represents Earth. Unless you are actually using it, it should be propped upright on your altar. Although you can buy wood or slate pentacles from occult shops, there are several ways to make one at home. The simplest is to use a pair of compasses to draw a circle on a piece of card, or draw around a saucer. Then cut out the circle and draw a five-pointed star within it and you have a basic pentacle ready for use.

Another way is to use an up-turned terracotta drainage saucer from a plant pot, and draw a pentagram on that. Or you could buy some modelling clay (the type that fires in a conventional oven) roll it into a disk, inscribe a pentagram on it and pop it in the oven. Choose an Earth colour such as green or brown.

This is the method I chose before I bought my wooden pentacle. You will need some sort of pentacle for the spells in this book.

the wand

The wand is what witches use to direct power. It represents the element of Air, and tradition states that it should reach from your inner elbow to the tip of your middle finger in length.

There are crystal wands available, but these can be expensive. My own wand was free. I found it lying on the path in front of me as I walked through a nearby wood. On picking up the fallen twig I found that it was exactly the right length, so I gave silent thanks to nature (talking to yourself in the woods can get you carried off by the men in white coats!) and took my new wand home with me. It has been on my altar and used in my spells ever since. I found my friend's wand for her in the same way – this time in my own garden. Try it for yourself. Go out into nature and silently ask for a wand to use in magic. Keep your eyes peeled and one will make itself known to you.

the chalice

The chalice can be any stemmed vessel and is used to represent the element of Water. A stemmed drinking glass is acceptable, but try to use one of coloured glass as this seems more magical. For a long time I used a lovely blue drinking glass with a long, elegant stem, which I bought from a kitchen reject shop for only £1. Now I am lucky enough to own a beautiful pewter chalice that is shaped into the face of a bearded tree spirit. This chalice looks wonderful on my altar and it is a pleasure to use in my rituals, but it is not essential to my magic. You must find a chalice that suits you and your finances. Use it to hold milk, juice or spring water during your rituals.

the athame

The athame is the ritual knife that witches use to direct strong power. It is also used to represent the Fire element. However, knives are potentially dangerous and it is, in any event, illegal in many countries to supply any blade to a person under 16 years of age, so don't even try to get hold of one. Instead use an old blunted paper knife or a knitting needle to inscribe things with, and a candle to represent Fire. I have never owned an athame and direct all my spells with my wand or my hand, so I suggest that you do the same.

the cauldron

The cauldron is used to mix things and as a tool of transformation. You could use an old saucepan or cooking pot, but make sure that it can withstand heat. You will need some kind of cauldron for the Lotions and Potions chapter of this book (see pages 57–68).

the broom

The broom is used for decoration and to sweep magical areas clean of negative energy. It is not essential for the spells of this book, but brooms can be bought cheaply from garden centres and flower shops if you like the idea.

phases of the moon

Witches work in tune with the phases of the moon, and moon magic is an integral part of the Craft. The moon holds a special power over our world; its magnetic force governs the tides of our waters and even influences the menstrual cycle of women.

A witch not only recognises and acknowledges this power, she also uses it to her own advantage by casting particular spells during a particular moon phase. The only exception to this rule is spells that are cast in an emergency, which are cast there and then, regardless of the moon phase. Here are the most significant moon phases and their uses in magic.

- **New moon:** appears as a thin sliver of light in the sky. All spells for new ventures, projects or new beginnings should be cast during this phase. The new moon is also good for spells concerning innocence, childhood and general cleansings.

- **Waxing moon:** as the moon grows from new to full. All spells that bring something into your life should be worked during this phase. It is particularly good for spells of growth and fertility.

- **Full moon:** this is the most powerful phase of the moon and all spells can be cast effectively during it. You should also be aware that you can use the night before and the night after this moon for magical workings, which gives you three whole nights of full-moon power!

✺ **Waning moon:** as the moon grows smaller in the sky. Witches use this phase to remove from their lives unhelpful influences, such as poverty, bad habits, negative people, bad relationships and so on. If you want gently to rid your life of something, then use the waning moon.

✺ **Dark moon:** when the moon is not visible in the sky. This is traditionally a time of rest, and the only magic worked during it is banishings (which pull someone or something away from you) and bindings (which freeze someone's or something's power and influence over you).

✺ **Blue moon:** a blue moon occurs when there is more than one full moon in a single calendar month. The second full moon is then classed as a blue moon. This is a time for setting long-term goals and casting spells to help you manifest your dreams. Blue-moon energy is rare and should never be wasted. You should always perform some type of goal-setting magic on this night.

Learn to recognise the different phases of the moon. Look for the moon in the night sky and notice how she appears to change with the different seasons. Most calendars and diaries now include moon phases, so find out what phase we are in now and begin to study the patterns. In time you will automatically know what phase the moon is in, just as you know what day of the week it is.

days of power

Just as the moon lends us different energies through her cycle, so too do the days of the week.

✺ **Monday:** as the name suggests, Monday is the moon day. Spells related to your home, pets and family, feminine issues, psychic development and dreams will be enhanced if performed on this day.

Tuesday: Mars rules this day, so it's good for any positive confrontation. Magic for business, work and getting your point across should be worked on a Tuesday, as should spells for courage and bravery, Mars being the god of war.

Wednesday: Wednesday is ruled by Mercury, the winged messenger, so all spells for communications and creativity should be cast on a Wednesday, as well as protection spells to keep telephones and computers in good working order.

Thursday: ruled by Jupiter, this is the day for money and prosperity spells, holiday and travel spells and for working towards educational goals. It's also a great day to study, so start that project!

Friday: this day belongs to Venus, so all spells for love, friends and socialising will be enhanced if you perform them on a Friday. It's also a good day to shop for clothes and make-up for a special occasion, so take advantage of those late-night shop opening hours.

Saturday: ruled by Saturn, this is a good day to pay back debts or magically call in money owed to you. It's also good for releasing negative thought patterns and overcoming bad habits.

Sunday: once again as the name suggests, Sunday is ruled by the sun. This is a fine day to begin an exercise programme, take a magical walk in nature (perhaps looking for your wand), plant a herb garden or meet up with friends. Sunday is also a good day for 'me time' with a good book, or for indulging in a favourite hobby.

magical colours

The following is a list of colours and their uses in magic. These colours can be related to any object used in magic, and you can even incorporate them into your wardrobe and make-up bag to give you a magical edge.

By choosing the correct colour correspondence and focusing on your need you will soon be making positive magic. This technique is especially good for candle magic.

- **Silver:** for spells of femininity, moon power and the night.

- **White:** for purity, cleansing, childhood, innocence, truth and protection.

- **Gold:** for masculinity, sun power and the daylight hours.

- **Yellow:** for communication, creativity, examinations, attraction and tests.

- **Green:** for finances, security, employment, career, fertility and luck.

- **Light blue:** for calmness, tranquillity, patience, understanding and good health.

- **Blue:** for healing, wisdom, dream interpretation, knowledge and dreamscaping (using your dreams in a magical way to solve problems, find answers and so on).

- **Pink:** for honour, friendship, virtue, morality, success and contentment.

- **Purple:** for power, meditation, psychic ability, mild banishings, ambition, inner strength, divinations and physical fitness.

- **Orange:** for adaptability, zest for life, social occasions, energy and imagination.

- **Brown:** for neutrality, stability, strength, grace, family, pets and decision-making.

- **Red:** for all matters of love and for courage in the face of adversity.

≋ **Grey:** for cancellations, greed, anger and envy.

≋ **Black:** for strong banishings, bindings, limitations, loss, confusion and defining boundaries.

Remember that these colour correspondences can be related to ribbons, thread, balloons, crayons, paints, candles, glitter and anything else you use in your spell-castings. There are many tools available for you to include in your magic.

herbs and incense

Witches use a variety of 'natural' tools. The most popular of these are herbs and spices, which are used in some of the spells in this book. I have suggested you use the dried variety, as they are so easy to borrow from the kitchen or buy in the supermarket, but if you have fresh herbs in the garden, or want to grow some on your window sill, that's fine. I have used only common herbs and spices, such as mint, basil, bay leaves, rosemary and cinnamon, so you won't have any trouble getting hold of the ones you need.

Witches also use essential oils and incense in spells. These can be bought from chemists, candle shops and department stores and are used in several ways. Oils can be used to anoint candles and talismans, or put in bath potions, oil burners, etc. Incense can be used to give a magical boost to practically any spell. You don't need to have a collection to start with. Lavender is the most commonly used, so perhaps you can treat yourself to a tiny bottle of that, and increase your collection as and when you need or want to.

Nothing could be simpler than adding herbs and oils to magical spells. In time you will be able to write your own spells and choose the appropriate herbs, oils, incenses and so on to give your spells more of a kick.

setting up an altar

We witches have special places in our homes where we cast spells and perform rituals. These places are called altars, and no two are ever the same. Creating an altar is a very individual process. If your friends are witches, the chances are that their altars will be very different from yours.

An altar is a place of power. It is where you gather your tools and make magic. It is a work table dedicated to witchcraft. Although an altar should be an expression of who you are, there are several things that most altars have in common.

Traditionally, an altar should be lit with candlelight only, so you should place two white candles at the back of the altar. These are called illuminator candles. The altar should also hold some representation of the four elements. This could be as simple as the tools we have already mentioned – for example, a pentacle for Earth, a chalice for Water, a wand for Air and a candle for Fire. In addition to these things you might want to represent the elements with something from the list below.

- **Earth:** pentacle, salt, soil, sand, a plant, fresh flowers, crystals, stones, a rock, a garden gnome or a dryad figure.

- **Air:** wand, feather, fan, incense, a photo of clouds, a wind instrument (pan pipes, flute, etc.), wind chimes, a figure of a bird or fairy, or a mythological creature with wings such as Pegasus or a griffin.

- **Fire:** athame, sword, candle, horse-shoe, lantern, fiery-coloured crystal, match, lava rock, picture of a desert or volcano, or a dragon statue.

- **Water:** chalice of water, bottle of aquamarine-coloured bath oil, a mirror, a water feature, sea-shells, wishing well, goldfish, dried starfish, a mermaid figure or doll, a statue of a dolphin or sea horse.

Decide where you would like to set up your altar. A window sill, a bookshelf, the top of a chest of drawers or a bedside table are all fine. Now clean the surface and set out the things you have collected for it. You might like to add flowers, or a photograph of your family or a pet. Make your altar represent yourself and your interests.

Traditionally the altar should be placed in the north, but when you are starting out the act simply of creating an altar is enough. In time, as you become more acquainted with the practice of the Craft, you can move your altar to the north by watching where the sun sets in relation to your room, or by using a compass.

You will probably find that you add to your altar as you move deeper into the Craft, placing on it beautiful figures of wood nymphs and fairies, or collections of pebbles and shells from the seaside. I have a lovely statue of a woodland dryad whose legs turn into the trunk of a tree. She stands in the centre of one of my altars and always makes me smile.

Keep your altar clean and tidy, as dust will affect your magic in a negative way. And lastly, always fill your chalice with fresh, clean water every day. This is your magical cup, and by keeping it full you are attracting a full and happy life.

casting a circle

To witches the area in which we work magic is known simply as the Circle. The area within the Circle is known as sacred space. Before every spell you cast or ritual you perform, you should always cast a Circle.

The Circle is the boundary that keeps all negative energies away from you and your magic. It also keeps the magic power within its 'walls' until the witch directs it towards its purpose. This is done by pointing the wand up and to the centre of the Circle, or by blowing out a candle or burning a spell paper and so on.

Here is how to cast a Circle:

- Stand with your arm outstretched and, pointing with your finger or your wand, walk around (or turn if the space is small) in a circle three times in a clockwise direction. The Wiccan term for clockwise is 'deosil'.

- Imagine a stream of blue light forming a circle around you.

- Now imagine that the light expands upwards and below you, forming a sphere of blue light. You and your altar are within this sphere. Clap once and say:

This Circle is sealed!

You are now ready to work your magic.

- After casting your spell, you should take down the Circle by moving around it in an anti-clockwise, or 'widdershins', direction. Feel the light being drawn back into your hand. Now clap once and say:

This Circle is open, but never broken.

This means that you have released the Circle, not destroyed it.

Finally you should release any magical energy that still lingers around you. Witches call this grounding. The best way to ground after magic is to lie flat on the floor for several minutes, allowing the energy to drain away. Then eat and drink something to re-balance your own energy.

You now have all the basic knowledge of witchcraft and are ready to perform your chosen spells. Remember to do so with clarity and a strong focus.

> *Come with Morgana, I'll show you the way*
> *Into a life of enchantment ...*
> *Come with Morgana, we'll cast spells today*
> *Our future will be full of magic ...*

Personal Spells and Rituals

At last, we've come to the good bit – spell-casting! That's what you're really reading this book for, isn't it?

In this chapter we will be looking at a series of simple yet effective spells that centre on you yourself. Here are spells for increasing confidence and releasing anger, plus enchantments, meditations and invocations.

have a good day spell

Cast this spell first thing in the morning for the best results. All you need is a glass of water and a mirror. The bathroom is probably the best place to work this spell, so lock the door behind you and fill the glass with cold water. To make the spell more powerful, use your magical chalice.

- **Stand before the mirror and say quietly to yourself:**

  I'm going to have a really good day.
  Today everything will go well. Today is
  going to be great!

- **Place your power hand (that's the one you write with) over the glass of water and imagine that you are sending magical white light into it. This is known as 'charging' a potion. Now look yourself in the eye in the mirror. Smile and say:**

  I take into myself the power of a truly
  magical day.

🦋 **Drink all the water and finish with the words:**

> *Blessed Be!*

Now wash and dress and generally go about preparing for the good day ahead.

happy spell

Everyone has days when they feel really down in the dumps. Sometimes this gives us a chance to retreat from life for a much-needed break. After all, without the lows, we wouldn't feel the highs. But we should always remember that we have power over our emotions and a simple spell can leave us feeling much better.

Music is a very powerful magical tool. For this spell you will need a tape or CD of your favourite music. It should be something with a beat, something to get your toes tapping and that you can sing along with. You will also need a clear quartz crystal – this has natural energising powers.

🦋 **Take the crystal in your receptive hand (this is the one you don't write with) and set the CD playing.**

🦋 **Feel the music, don't just listen.**

🦋 **At the same time, feel the coolness of the crystal in your hand, maybe making your skin feel cold or begin to tingle – this is the energy of the crystal being absorbed by your body.**

🦋 **Allow the music and the crystal to uplift you, to energise you. Sing along, dance, allow yourself to be happy.**

Afterwards, run the crystal under the cold tap for a minute or two to cleanse it and leave it to dry in natural sunlight. Keep it on your altar or with your CD so that you can use it again when you need it.

to release your own anger

Anger is a natural emotion. We all feel it. If we didn't, we wouldn't be human – we'd be androids! But unless you release your anger, it will just build up inside, creating more and more negative feeling until it bursts out when you least expect it. When you are angry about something, try this spell to release your anger.

🌾 **Put on some sweat clothes and your running shoes and go jogging. No kidding! Exercise is a healthy release for all negative emotions, especially when it is backed up with a little magic.**

🌾 **As you run, imagine you are running away from your anger and repeat this charm in your head:**

> *As I run, anger be gone.*
> *Leave it behind, for no one to find.*

🌾 **Keep running and mentally chanting until you feel you have left all your anger behind. This spell can be adapted to release any negative emotion.**

It's a sad fact that there are many dangerous people about. For safety's sake, don't run anywhere where you might be vulnerable – the spell will work just as well if you run around the block or around your own garden. And give the dog a run too!

to calm anger in someone else

If a parent, friend or teacher is angry with you for some reason, try this little witchy trick. Firstly, don't argue back. This is not the time to put your point across, and angry people don't listen anyway. Wait until the person has calmed down and gently and politely make your point in a day or two. A true witch knows when to speak and when to be silent.

Now imagine the angry person being surrounded by a

calming blue bubble of light. This light is part of the universal power that is all around us. Also imagine a large mirror between this person and yourself. This mirror deflects any negative energy away from you. Alternatively, you could place your watch so that the glass face is pointing in their direction and this will have the same effect. The angry person should calm down or leave the room. For the best results, use this technique as soon as tempers become frayed.

to bind a personal belonging

This spell will ensure that something you lend will come back to you.

- Before you lend an item, say a book or a CD, take it to your altar and leave it there for one hour so that it becomes a part of your magic.

- Then go back to it and take with you a long black ribbon. Wrap the ribbon around the item and tie it loosely in a bow like a present.

- Repeat the following chant three times:

    What's yours is yours, what's mine is mine,
    With this ribbon I draw the line.
    To (name of lender) this (name of object)
        is lent,
    With it the magic of the Craft is sent
    To ensure this book returns to me.
    This is my will – so mote it be!

- Gently, without undoing the bow, remove the ribbon from the item and place it on your altar. Lend the item to your friend and when it is safely returned undo the knot of the ribbon and acknowledge your power.

to overcome shyness

For this spell you will need a tissue or handkerchief, a bottle of violet essential oil and a packet of violet sweets. Violets have long been thought of as shy flowers and so they will help to strengthen the spell.

- Take all three items to your altar and lay them out in a row.

- Light the candles on your altar as a sign that you are about to work magic.

- Think about your shyness and what situations have been the most difficult for you – reading aloud in class, for example, or talking to a boy. For me, drama class was a total nightmare!

- Now imagine yourself in those situations but without your shyness holding you back. Imagine that everything you say not only comes out right, but has everyone around you simply enthralled – including the boys!

- Hold that thought as you eat a violet sweet and then splash two or three drops of violet oil on to your handkerchief.

- Place the sweets and handkerchief together and, using your wand, draw a pentagram in the air, directly over them, and say:

  > *I enchant these items magically to relieve me of my shyness. So be it.*

- Blow out the candles.

Take the handkerchief and sweets to school with you and try really hard to overcome your shyness, knowing that you have magic on your side. Keep sniffing the handkerchief (if necessary, pretend you have a cold!) to remind you of your spell.

Whenever you feel you have done particularly well, reward yourself with a violet sweet at break time. Cast this spell as often as you need to and you will soon have your shyness under control.

To enhance this spell, add a few drops of violet oil to your bath water.

to increase confidence

This spell can be worked by itself or in addition to the one above. You will need a picture of someone you admire. This could be a family member, a fictional character or a movie star.

- **Sit quietly by your altar and look at the picture, thinking about what you admire most about the person.**

- **Then imagine how you could incorporate these traits into yourself. There's no need to dye your hair, change your accent or dial a plastic surgeon. All you need do is use the small details – which are usually the best ones anyway.**

- **Perhaps your idol smiles a lot – that's a fantastic way of making you feel good and look confident. Maybe they have a great sense of body language and carry themselves tall and straight, appearing to fill a room even though they're only five feet tall. Alternatively, they may have a skill that simply oozes confidence – the gift of the gab, a charming manner or even kick-boxing (think Buffy!) and so on.**

- **Once you realise what makes this person so attractive and confident, try on these traits for yourself. To be confident, the first thing you must do is think confident.**

- **Draw a pentagram on the back of the picture and keep it on your altar as a magical reminder.**

moving on

So far our spells have been very simple, using imagination and mental awareness as our main tools. Now we're going to move on to something slightly more complex. The following spells include specific moon phases and correspondences where appropriate, in addition to the mental techniques you have already learned.

to enchant a crystal

What you want: to enchant a crystal to your own specific needs.

What you need: your pentacle, a pen and paper, a snowy or clear quartz crystal (or a crystal the colour of which matches your purpose).

Moon time: full.

Enchanting a crystal means instilling it with the power to attract something good into your life, such as love, money, good health and so on.

- On the night of the full moon, cleanse your crystal by running it under the cold tap for about a minute. Carefully dry the crystal using a soft towel. Take care not to drop it as crystals are delicate and can scratch and chip quite easily.

- Now go to your altar and light the illuminator candles.

- Place your pentacle in the middle of the altar and on a piece of paper write the words:

  I charge this crystal with the power of ...
  (state your magical goal). *So mote it be!*

- Place this paper on the pentacle and put the crystal on top.

- You now need to chant your magical goal. So if you are enchanting a crystal for love, you would chant:

    Love, love, bring me love.

    Continue to chant for as long as you can remain focused.

- Then blow out the candles and leave the crystal in place for 24 hours.

After this time, your crystal is ready to use either by itself to attract your magical goal, in which case you would carry it with you, or as a correspondence in a larger spell or ritual. If you choose to carry the crystal with you as a charm, you will need to repeat this spell and recharge it every full moon.

to release frustration and stress

What you want: to relieve yourself of these negative feelings.
What you need: a black candle, a candle holder, matches, black pepper, a sheet of kitchen towel, sunflower oil.
Moon time: waning.

- First take the black candle and empower it in the following way:

- Hold the candle firmly in both hands and imagine all your stress and frustration is being absorbed by the wax. If you like, you can lift the candle close to your lips and 'breathe' the frustration into it.

- Now dip your finger in the sunflower oil and rub it all over the candle, beginning in the centre and working outwards to both ends.

↙ Next, pour a little black pepper on to the kitchen towel and roll the candle through it until it is completely covered in pepper. Black pepper has excellent banishing powers and will help to relieve you of your frustration. If the pepper makes you sneeze, then simply imagine that you are sneezing your stress away.

↙ Put the candle in the holder and light it. Allow it to burn down and work its magic, but keep it away from anything flammable. You could place it in the bath for safety.

Be very careful when you are using candles and matches, and always take the appropriate safety precautions.

spell for inner strength

We all have an inner strength that helps us through the rotten days we all have to cope with now and then. Sometimes you may feel the need to increase or magically invoke your inner strength. The following ritual will help you to do just that.

You will need to be in a place with trees, so go to a park or woods or simply use a tree in your own garden. Any kind of tree can be used for this spell, but an oak tree is especially good as oaks are magically symbolic of great strength. Take with you a pouch full of nuts, seeds and raisins. This is your offering pouch.

↙ After finding a tree you like and feel comfortable with, sit beneath the branches and lean your back on the tree trunk. At this point you should begin to feel calm and relaxed, perhaps without knowing exactly why. Trees have this effect on us. You have entered into this particular tree's space, so you are sharing its positive energy.

- ✍ Now close your eyes and in your mind begin to talk to the tree spirit, asking if you can share its strength so that you can deal with whatever challenges you are currently experiencing. Feel free to tell the tree spirit your worries and problems.

- ✍ Then sit quietly, breathing in the energy around the tree, and listen carefully for any words that suddenly flit through your mind, as these could be a reply from the tree spirit.

- ✍ Feel the strength of the tree trunk down the length of your spine and magically take in this strength by imagining that your spine resembles your own inner tree.

- ✍ After a while you should feel more ready to face your problems and take on the world. At this point you can end your visualisation and know that your magic has worked.

- ✍ Spend a little longer with the tree and enjoy being out in the fresh air among natural things. When you are ready to leave, thank the tree spirit and empty your offering pouch at the roots of the tree for the wildlife to enjoy. This completes the exchange of energy.

When you are back in your normal everyday routine and feel the need to call on your new inner strength, simply recall the visualisation of your time spent with the tree spirit.

broomstick meditation

Meditation is a mental journey which can be used to help you to relax or to find solutions to current challenges in your life. The following meditation is a form of astral journey and a relaxation technique. It is also a lot of fun.

- ✎ **Begin by lying down on your back on the bed or the floor. If you like, you can have incense burning or soft relaxing music playing in the background. Alternatively, you might prefer the fresh air from an open window and absolute silence.**

- ✎ **Once you are settled comfortably, begin to relax each part of your body, beginning at your feet and working up your body.**

- ✎ **When you are fully relaxed, from feet to head, count slowly down from ten to one, and imagine that with each number you are going further and further into a deep, dark wood.**

- ✎ **When you reach number one, you are in a clearing in the forest and before you, hovering in the air at hip level, is a magic broomstick.**

- ✎ **Go over to the broomstick, introduce yourself by your magical name, and then climb on, so that the brush of the broom is behind you.**

- ✎ **Take hold of the broom stave and say:**

  Let us fly!

- ✎ **Now feel yourself ascending on the magical broomstick and watch as the forest disappears beneath you. Feel the wind in your hair as you fly through the night sky. Your magical journey has now begun and you can use the broomstick to take you wherever you would like to go. You could nip over to your best friend's house and peek in her** bedroom window to see what she is doing. Or you could go to your grandmother's to check that she is okay. Perhaps a little more adventure suits you? If so, fly the broomstick to a magical place such as Stonehenge or Glastonbury, or anywhere else you have always wanted to go. This is an astral journey and there are no limitations.

When you are ready to come out of your meditation, fly back to the grove in the forest and land your broomstick carefully.

Know that it will be here waiting for you whenever you would like to 'escape' for a while. Now walk back through the wood, counting up from one to ten. At ten open your eyes. Lie still a moment or two and think about the mental journey you have just taken. Ground yourself (perhaps by putting your hands and forehead on the floor or by eating something) and then go about your day.

Look Good, Feel Great!

In the last chapter we looked at the simple side of spell-casting, which should have served to whet your appetite! From now on the spells and rituals will become progressively more advanced.

Always remember that your mind is the greatest magical tool you will ever possess. You should master the techniques of visualisation and mental awareness by performing magic on a regular basis. The more you practise, the better you will get, and you will then be able to design and create your own spells.

In this chapter we will be working with spells that will help you to feel more confident in your looks and to become more aware of your body language. It's important to realise that while we can't all look like film stars or glamorous super-models, we can all be beautiful, as true beauty radiates from the inside out. And we should also remember that Hollywood stars have a whole team of people *making* them look that good. If you had an entire workforce of make-up artists, fashion gurus, hair stylists and lighting men at your disposal, you'd look like a beauty queen, too.

spell for calm

Finding an inner sense of peace and calm is the first step towards true beauty.

> **What you want:** to feel completely calm.
> **What you need:** a blue candle, lavender oil, a CD of soothing music, such as Enya.
> **Moon time:** new.

- Go to your altar and light the illuminator candles.

- Sit for a moment and let go of all the day's stresses and disappointments.

- Concentrate on your breathing. Breathe in for a count of three, visualising yourself breathing in pure white light. Now breathe out for a count of four and see this breath as red smoke or vapour. This is an excellent way of releasing all your stress and anxieties. Continue until you feel you have released all the negative energies.

- Now put the soothing music on softly in the background. Take the blue candle and rub a little lavender oil on to it. Light the wick and enjoy the scent. Rub a little more lavender oil on to each of your temples and the pulse points at your wrists. Rub any excess oil into your hands.

- Sit quietly, meditating upon the flame of the candle and enjoying your new-found sense of peace and calm. Allow the candle to fill the room with the scent of lavender and then snuff out the flame.

Perform this spell on each new moon for maximum effect.

spell for energy

What you want: to increase your energy.
What you need: a healthy balanced meal, your visualisation skills.
Moon time: any – use daily at meal times.

- Make sure that everything on your plate is healthy, nutritious food. Fruit, vegetables and unprocessed carbohydrates all help to give us an energy boost.

- First, draw a pentagram (a five-pointed star) over the plate of food. You can use your wand or your finger, or if people are around, simply see it in your mind's eye.

- Next, silently give thanks to the nature spirits for the gift of this food and ask that by eating it you will increase your energy level.

- Now enjoy the meal, savouring each mouthful and the different textures and tastes. Make the meal a magical tool and a way of taking in energy.

- When you have finished your meal, thank whoever cooked it for you. Tell them how much you enjoyed it so that they know their work is appreciated. Alternatively, if you are in the dining hall at school, give silent thanks to the cook and then go about your day.

spell for inner beauty

We all have an inner beauty, and the main trick in bringing it out is realising that it's there. To help us in this quest we use an image or symbol of Aphrodite, the goddess of love and beauty (her Roman name is Venus). This image could be a figure brought back from abroad, a picture you have drawn or one from a book, or a scallop shell, which also symbolises this goddess who came from the sea.

What you want: to bring your inner beauty to the surface.

What you need: a white candle, a representation of Aphrodite, a special item that represents true beauty to you, such as a flower, a crystal or a photograph of your mother.

Moon time: waxing.

- Take the representation of Aphrodite to your altar, and place it on your pentacle.

- Then put the lighted candle and your special item of beauty on either side of the pentacle.

- Place your hands, palms upwards, at each side of the images and say the following charm three times:

> *I call upon sweet Aphrodite*
> *To help me find my inner beauty.*
> *Beauty from the inside out*
> *Helps me to release self-doubt.*
> *As above, so below,*
> *I radiate an inner glow.*
> *My inner beauty all shall see,*
> *As I will, so shall it be!*

- Sit for a few minutes and think of all the things that make you a beautiful person: courage, integrity, a willingness to help others, a sense of humour, intelligence, a listening ear, a quick smile, a ready laugh, etc.

- Know that you will always be beautiful and know that you now have the power of the Craft to enhance that beauty.

- Snuff out the candle and put your things away. Perform this spell whenever you are feeling bad about yourself, or just to give an added boost to your confidence.

spell for feeling glamorous

Glamour is a state of mind. If you believe you are glamorous, then others will see you in that way. Witches use a particular type of spell to help us in our quest for improved appearance. These spells are called, appropriately enough, 'glamories'. If a witch wants to appear confident and strong when she is actually quaking in her boots, then she will cast a glamour spell. If she wants to appear slightly imposing, she will cast a glamorie and work on her posture. Glamories can be directed towards any aspect of your appearance. They are an illusion, formed by the web of magic. Glamories don't last unless performed on a regular basis.

I have used glamories over and over again and can vouch for their effectiveness. On one occasion I was going on a blind date that my best friend and her boyfriend had set up. I was very nervous, so I cast a glamour spell around myself so that I would appear strong, confident, magical and mysterious. It worked far better than I had planned, as my friend later told me that both my date and hers had confessed to being terrified of me! But I felt totally in control all evening.

Glamories do work, so use them wisely. The following is a general glamour spell, but you can adapt it to any aspect of your personal appearance you wish to improve.

> **What you want:** to increase feelings of glamour and to perform a glamorie.
> **What you need:** a special hand mirror, spring water.
> **Moon time:** full.

On the night of the full moon, take the hand mirror and spring water outside or to a window from which you can see the moon. I generally use a Victorian silver hand mirror for glamour spells, but you can use any mirror that is large enough to reflect your whole face and small enough to hold in your hands.

- ⚬ Place the mirror on the floor so that it reflects the moon.

- ⚬ Now think of the change you would like to make, for instance to appear taller, slimmer or just more glamorous in general.

- ⚬ Dip your finger in the spring water and write the desired change upon the mirror's surface. Continue to focus on your glamour goal, take up the mirror and repeat this chant three times:

> *Witches' power, witches' wheel,*
> *Illusion will be seen as real.*
> *The change I desire will come to pass,*
> *As this magical spell I cast.*
> *Behold, I gaze in the magic mirror,*
> *And see the light of glamour shimmer.*
> *Witch's skill and witch's power,*
> *A glamorie's cast from this hour!*

Keep this mirror only for your magical spells. A glamorie will generally last around 24 hours, so repeat the spell as necessary. You can cast this spell using the light of a white candle instead of the moonlight if you wish. This is often necessary during the waning and dark moons, and it means that you can cast a glamorie spell whenever you need one.

Look Good, Feel Great!

to look your best

What you want: to enchant your clothes with magic.

What you need: all your clothes, your wand, a solution of spring water mixed with 10 drops of rose geranium essential oil in a spritzer bottle.

Moon time: full.

First sort out your wardrobe and throw anything you don't wear into bags for the charity shop – or have a clothes-swapping party with your friends. This will make room for new clothes!

Now pile all your clothes in a heap. Don't forget your underwear.

Next, cast a Circle around yourself and your clothes. Take up the spritzer bottle and begin to spray the solution in the air over your clothes. Now say the following:

> *Skirts and tops and bras and pants,*
> *Jeans and dresses, I now enchant.*
> *With this potion I spray with zest,*
> *To make me always look my best!*

With your wand, draw a pentagram in the air above the clothes.

Take down your Circle and put the clothes away neatly.

Finally, draw a pentagram on your wardrobe door with your finger.

Repeat the spell with shoes and accessories.

spell for great hair

This spell works in a similar way to the one above, in that you are enchanting something with magic. In this case, you are enchanting all the things you use to keep your hair looking good.

What you want: magically to enhance your hair care routine.

What you need: all your hair care products, your hair brushes and combs, sea salt, 1 metre/1 yard of ribbon in your favourite colour.

Moon time: waxing.

Gather together your hair brush, drier and all your hair care products, such as shampoo, conditioner, hair spray, mousse, etc. Place them all in the centre of your altar and, using the sea salt, sprinkle an unbroken circle around them. Now tie all the products together with the ribbon and say:

I enchant these products with the gift of beautiful-looking hair.
May my hair always be healthy, shiny and clean. So mote it be!

Now leave all the items together for 24 hours, after which you should scoop up the salt and bury it in the garden.

To enhance this spell, regularly use one of the hair potions from the Lotions and Potions chapter (see pages 57–68).

to lose weight and keep to a healthy diet

What you want: magic help to stay on a healthy diet.

What you need: modelling clay, a box, a piece of black fabric, a piece of white fabric, 1 metre/1 yard of black ribbon, 1 metre/1 yard of white ribbon, an inscribing tool, a copy of the diet plan.

Moon time: begin the diet on a waning moon.

- First of all make sure that your diet plan is healthy and balanced – starvation doesn't look good on anyone.

- Next, take the modelling clay and with it fashion two simple, doll-like figures. Witches call these figures poppets. Make sure that one poppet is slightly larger and rounder than the other.

- Now take the largest poppet and inscribe on its tummy the weight you are now. Be truthful – lying to yourself isn't witch-like.

- Now wrap this poppet in the black fabric and place it in the box – an old shoe-box will do. Seal the box by binding it with the black ribbon and then place the whole thing in a cupboard or drawer that you seldom use. The idea is to remove it from sight.

- Now take the thinner poppet and inscribe on this your goal weight. Be realistic – 45 kg/100 lb is not healthy for a growing girl. Place this second poppet on your altar where you can see it everyday to remind you of your goal.

In addition, always begin your diet on a waning moon. To enhance your chances of success, drink plenty of the Sun and

Moon Waters described in the Lotions and Potions chapter (pages 57–8).

Once you have reached your goal weight, bury the larger poppet in the earth. Wrap the thinner poppet in the white fabric, place it in the box and seal the box with the white ribbon. This will help you to maintain your ideal weight.

a simple healing spell

What you want: to send healing energy to yourself or another.

What you need: a white or blue candle, an inscribing tool, lavender essential oil, a pentacle.

Moon time: new to full.

- **On the candle, carefully inscribe the name of the person who is ill. If you are doing this ritual to help heal someone else, then you will need to get their permission first. Witches never work for anyone without their agreement – this is a very important ethical rule of Wicca.**

- **Next, anoint the candle with lavender essential oil, a well-known 'heal all' oil. Place the candle in a holder and put it on your pentacle.**

- **Light the wick and visualise a healing white light surrounding yourself or whoever is ill. Continue with the visualisation for as long as your focus is strong.**

- **Allow the candle to burn down.**

the 'look at me!' spell

What you want: to get yourself noticed.
What you need: a picture of yourself that you don't want (as this is a fire spell), a hair clipping, an unusual item of clothing or jewellery or an accessory, your favourite perfume, your cauldron, a pentacle, matches.
Moon time: full.

- On the night of the full moon take all the above items to your altar.

- Place the photograph of yourself in the cauldron.

- Now put your hair clipping on top of the photo.

- Next, place your unusual item or accessory on the pentacle, along with your favourite perfume. They will now be charged with magical energy.

- Carefully set light to the photograph and hair (you might want to do this part in the kitchen sink) and say these words as they burn:

  Power of the witches rise,
  Light the flame and draw the eyes.
  This image of myself I burn;
  I cast this spell to make heads turn.
  The flame of magic takes my hair,
  So people will turn round and stare.
  Noticed, seen and centre be!
  No longer such a nobody!
  Attention given pleasantly,
  Look at me! So mote it be!

- When the flame has died, scatter the ashes in the garden. The following day, wear the unusual item and a little of the perfume.

To connect this with the Spell for Great Hair (see page 50), spray a little of the perfume on your hair brush.

healing basket

If you know someone who is ill but you are unable to work magic for them, for whatever reason, then you could consider making them a healing basket. You will need a medium-sized basket which you should line with blue fabric. Now fill the basket with anything that suggests healing. Here are a few hints: blue and violet candles, lavender essential oil, aromatherapy bath salts, a few sachets of herbal tea, a tape or CD of nature sounds such as dolphins or whale song, a self-help book, a good novel, some favourite chocolates and so on. Tie blue and purple ribbons around the basket to make it look pretty and deliver it with a get well card and a smile.

angel healing

What you want: to invoke the aid of the angel of healing.

What you need: a white tea-light and holder, a representation of an angel, such as a picture, a statue or a tiny pin or brooch of an angel (or you could simply use a white feather).

Moon time: full.

- Place your angel representation on your altar.

- Place the tea-light in its holder in front of the angel and light it. Now call on Raphael, the 'shining healer', and ask for his help in the following way:

> *Angel of healing, angel of light,*
> *Take away this endless night.*
> *I call on you, Raphael,*
> *To heal the one I love so well.*
> *Let not this illness last too long,*
> *But bring back health with a healing*
>   *song.*

> *Angel of healing, angel of light,*
> *Put an end to this illness, let health be*
> * in sight.*
> *So mote it be!*

- Concentrate on good health being given to yourself or your loved one. Visualise a happy outcome for everyone.

- Allow the candle to burn out and give thanks to Raphael. Give the angel representation to the person who is ill as a charm to connect them to your spell.

first blood rite

With your first period, you move from the stage of girlhood to that of young woman. This is a major transition in your life, and you might like to mark the occasion in some way.

This ritual, known as a first blood rite, will be one that you yourself create. It is your rite and it should be as individual as you are. The following is simply a guideline. The most important thing to remember is that this is a time of celebration. Menstruation is not a curse; it is a most magical time. Witches see it as a time when we are at our most powerful, and some serious magic can be worked during the 'moon blood', as witches call it.

You can turn this rite into a small party, inviting friends – but only those who have already begun their own cycle. Or it could be a family affair (girls only), with your mother and aunts and so on. Alternatively, you could create a private rite for yourself alone.

> **What you want:** to welcome womanhood.
> **What you need:** red candles, red wine, sherry or port (but ask your parents first), nibbles, a gift to acknowledge this new phase of your life.
> **Moon time:** any – perform during your first period.

- The colour of the ritual should be red, for obvious reasons, so wear red if you can, light red candles and (if you are allowed) celebrate the occasion with a glass of red wine. Pour a little of this into the earth and slowly sip the rest.

- Enjoy the nibbles, reflect on the change you have undergone and (if family and friends are present) listen to what the older women have to say about the best things in being a woman.

- Finally, receive some form of gift, either from yourself or from a close female relative or friend. This could be a pretty bag to keep essential sanitary items in, or perhaps make-up or a piece of jewellery – something to mark the fact that you have now moved from childhood to womanhood.

If you have already begun your monthly periods but have not yet acknowledged this in some way, then simply perform this rite during your next period.

Look Good, Feel Great!

Lotions and Potions

When people think of witchcraft they tend to think of bubbling cauldrons and pungent potions, and that's exactly what we're going to create in this chapter.

Most witches have the ability to rustle up a quick potion or a healing bath remedy. I have to admit that as far as cooking is concerned I'm useless, but when it comes to making potions, lotions and magical brews I can happily spend hours at the stove and enjoy every minute.

There's a bit of the kitchen witch in all of us I think. In this chapter you will find recipes for home-made beauty products, bath oils and crystals, massage oil blends and, of course, potions. No spell book would be complete without those.

The main point to remember is that these home-made remedies are free from all preservatives, so they don't last. Therefore, you should make only as much as you need – the amounts given here are generally enough for a single application for one person. As you gain in experience, you may like to begin experimenting using these recipes as a guideline. But always remember that herbs and essential oils are powerful products of nature, so seek advice from your local herbalist, or buy a good herbal book such as *A Wiccan Herbal* by Marie Rodway, published by Foulsham.

sun and moon waters

Water that has been empowered with magic can be used for all sorts of things. You can add it to your bath, use it as a hair rinse or make it the basis of a potion, as it is very beneficial to drink. Magical waters are easy to make, and use two natural sources of power – the sun and the moon. For the best results, use the night of the full moon and a day when the sun is strong, warm and bright. The midsummer solstice is an excellent time to make a magical sun water, and this should be specially labelled 'Solstice Sun Water' to distinguish it from any other sun waters you may have.

To make these magical waters you will need a 2-litre/ 3⅓-pint bottle of pure spring water, and two empty glass bottles that each hold 1 litre/1¾ pints. Divide the spring water between the two bottles and leave the first bottle out in the full light of the sun. You will have to keep moving the bottle as the sun crosses the sky to make sure your water gets the strongest power possible. If this is inconvenient simply put the bottle out at the time of the sun's strongest power, midday. Label the bottle 'Sun Water' and place it near your altar.

Now repeat this process on the night of the full moon, placing the second bottle out in the moon's most radiant beams. Again, leave the bottle out in the moon-light for as long as you possibly can, and then label it 'Full Moon Water'. Place this bottle by your altar also. Both waters are now fully charged and are ready to be used in your magic.

rainbow waters

Witches are fully aware of the powerful effects that various colours have on us, and we use these colours in our magic. One of the ways witches harness the power of colour is by making rainbow waters. Rainbow waters are just as simple to make as sun and moon waters, and again they can be used in a variety of ways in spell-casting.

You will need several empty bottles or jars and as many different food colourings as you can find. Now simply fill the bottles with spring water and add the food colouring until you get the depth of colour that you like. Now the waters can be used for magical purposes. For example, red water can be used in love potions, blue water can be added to a healing bath, and green water can be used to water the house plants or garden. Use the colour chart on pages 25–6 as a guide. Rainbow waters should be left near or on your altar to help charge their powers.

black tea hair rinse

This tea is for red or dark hair.

- Pour about **600 ml/1 pint of water into a pan and bring it to the boil. Add a tea bag and allow to steep for a few minutes.**

- **Use a spoon to scoop out the tea bag, then leave the tea to cool. Shampoo and condition your hair as usual.**

- **Then hold your hands over the tea hair rinse and empower it by saying:**

    With this tea
    My hair will be
    Strong and glossy for all to see.

- **Pour the rinse into a bowl of warm water and using a jug pour it over your hair again and again, gently massaging it in.**

- **After using the rinse, pour the water away into the earth to nourish the garden.**

lemon hair rinse

For all you lucky blondes out there!

- **Make and use this rinse in exactly the same way as the one above, but add 30 ml/2 tbsp of lemon juice instead of tea.**

- **Empower the rinse with the following words:**

    Lemon juice and lemon zest,
    My hair will always look its best!

strawberry face mask

What you need: 15 ml/1 tbsp crushed oats, two large strawberries, single cream.

> First grind the oats with a mortar and pestle.

> Next crush the strawberries until they are a soft pulp.

> Pour the oats and strawberries into your magical cauldron and add enough single cream to make the whole thing into a paste.

> Apply the face mask to your face and neck and leave for 15–20 minutes.

> Rinse off, pat dry, then apply a mild moisturiser.

egg white face mask

What you need: three large eggs.

> First separate the egg whites from the yolks. To do this, hold the egg over a bowl, break it carefully, then pour the yolk from one half of the shell to the other, allowing the white to fall into the bowl.

> Pour the whites into your cauldron, and put the yolks into a small hole in the garden to nourish the earth.

> Now whisk the egg whites until they become quite stiff and can be firmed into peaks. They should look something like meringue.

> Apply this mask to your face and neck and leave for about 15 minutes or until the mask has set.

> Then rinse the mask off with cool water, pat dry and apply a light moisturiser.

bath potion to heal aches and pains

Please note that magical bath potions should not be used with chemical bubble baths, oils and so on.

What you need: blue water; lavender, sandlewood and clary sage essential oils; sea salt.

ʃ **In your cauldron mix five drops of each oil with the blue water. Sprinkle in 5 ml/1 tsp of sea salt and mix it all together with your wand.**

ʃ **Make the sign of the pentagram above the bowl and then take the potion with you to the bathroom.**

ʃ **Spend a little time creating a healing atmosphere, perhaps bathing by the light of a blue candle.**

ʃ **Just before you step into the bath, add the potion from your cauldron. As soon as the oils merge with the hot water, their powerful, healing fragrances will be released.**

ʃ **Relax in the bath and allow the magic to work.**

lotion to ease a cold

What you need: 10 ml/2 tsp sunflower oil, five drops of eucalyptus essential oil, three drops of peppermint oil.
Moon time: prepare on a waning moon if possible.

ʃ **Pour the sunflower oil into a dark glass bottle and add the eucalyptus oil and the peppermint oil one drop at a time. Screw the cap on to the bottle and shake the mixture well. This potion should smell quite strongly, with the menthol fragrance of eucalyptus.**

- Leave the lotion on your pentacle for 24 hours to charge.

- Apply the lotion to your chest and throat and rub a little into your temples.

- You can also sprinkle a small amount on to a handkerchief or burn a few drops in a lamp ring or oil burner.

tea-tree and witch hazel spot blaster

What you need: a small dark glass bottle (an empty medicine bottle will do), a small bottle of witch hazel liquid, tea-tree essential oil.

Moon time: full.

- Clean the medicine bottle thoroughly. Pour into it 30 ml/2 tbsp of witch hazel and add 6 drops of pure essential tea-tree oil. Cap the bottle and give it a really good shake.

- Now place the potion on a window sill in the light of the full moon and leave it there as the moon wanes.

- At the time of the dark moon, take up the bottle and say:

> *As the moon wanes from full to dark,*
> *So my spots will wither and disappear!*

- Apply the potion, using clean cottonwool balls, to any spots you have.

- Use daily until your skin has cleared, and resume use if you feel a new blemish appearing.

To enhance this spell steam your face at least once a week over a bowl of hot water to which you have added three drops of tea-tree essential oil.

aromatherapy massage oil for PMT

What you need: 30 ml/2 tbsp almond oil, six drops of rose geranium essential oil, two drops of lavender essential oil, three drops of jasmine essential oil, a pink ribbon (optional), rose petals (optional).
Moon time: prepare at full moon.

⚅ Make this potion at the full moon and then use it whenever you are experiencing a painful period. Keep the potion in a cool dark place, away from direct sunlight and it will last quite well.

⚅ Mix all the ingredients in a dark glass blending bottle, then cap the bottle and give it a good shake.

⚅ Leave it overnight in the light of the moon.

⚅ The next day, add a few rose petals to the mixture and shake again. Tie a pretty pink ribbon around the neck of the bottle. Pink is the colour of self-love, and this ribbon will remind you to take care of yourself and pamper yourself a little at this time.

⚅ Use the oil to gently massage your tummy and lower back. This potion is also very effective at relieving any breast tenderness associated with PMT if massaged into this area – and can even help to ease growing pains if used daily.

⚅ Alternatively, add a little of the potion to your bath water, lie back and relax.

magical bath salts

What you need: a large box of Epsom salts, food colouring conducive to your magical purpose, essential oils conducive to your magical purpose (no more than three).

- Pour the salts into your cauldron and add the food colouring a few drops at a time. Mix really well until the salts are evenly coloured.

- Next, add the essential oil or oils of your choice – a maximum of 20 drops in all should be used.

- Transfer the bath salts into an attractive bottle or jar and, holding the jar in your hands, charge the salts to their magical purpose by chanting and focusing hard on your goal – for example, healing, love, attraction and so on. Hold your focus for as long as possible.

- Tie a pretty label to the jar, stating its new magical use – 'Healing Bath Salts', for example. Add these salts to your bath whenever you need their magic.

quick remedies for period pain

Indian potion: take 10 ml/2 tsp of Indian Brandy (available from pharmacies) in half a glass of hot water. Sweeten with a spoonful of sugar.

Peppermint potion: for this potion you can use either a little peppermint cordial mixed with hot water, or make a mug of peppermint herbal tea. Whichever method you choose, add two or three drops of Olive Bach flower remedy, as this will help you to overcome feelings of weariness (PMT can often leave you feeling drained of energy).

sycamore skin tonic

For this tonic, you will need to gather some leaves from a local tree, taking care that it isn't one growing by the roadside as this will, unfortunately, be polluted. First, silently ask the dryad if she can spare some leaves for your magic. Wait a few minutes and if all seems well, carefully pluck a few leaves and thank them. However, if you feel uncomfortable or a little panicky, this means that the dryad has said no, for nature's own reasons, and you should find another tree. Always leave an offering of nuts and seeds at the tree's roots whatever answer the dryad gives. This will strengthen your connection with nature.

> **What you need:** six large sycamore leaves, mortar and pestle, 600 ml/1 pint spring water, 15 ml/1 tbsp apple cider vinegar.

- Once you have gathered your leaves, take them home and wash them thoroughly.

- Now grind them to a pulp using a mortar and pestle, then put them into a pan, together with the spring water, and simmer gently on a low heat for about 20–30 minutes.

- Next, strain the leaf water into a jar and return the pulp to the Earth.

- Add the apple cider vinegar to the leaf water, cap the jar and shake well.

- Use the potion as a skin tonic, applying it with cottonwool morning and evening after washing. If kept refrigerated this sycamore skin tonic will last about seven days. Any remaining tonic should be added to your bath on the seventh day and a fresh preparation made.

love potion

This potion and the following ones in this chapter use a selection of Bach flower remedies, which are available from most large chemists and health food shops.

Although there are no potions in the world to make someone love you, 'love' potions have been used for centuries to help gain the attention of one you admire. This is just such a potion and uses the two key ingredients of any love potion – rose and honey. And there's a dash of wild oat for good measure.

> **What you need:** one raspberry herbal tea-bag, 2.5 ml/½ tsp golden honey, three drops of Wild Rose Bach flower remedy, three drops of Wild Oat Bach flower remedy.
>
> **Moon time:** full.

§ **First boil the kettle and steep the herbal tea-bag for about five minutes.**

§ **Next add the honey and the flower remedies. Stir in a deosil (clockwise) direction and repeat the following charm three times:**

> *By wild rose and raspberry,*
> *By wild oats and golden honey,*
> *By the notion of this potion,*
> *Love will be, so notice me!*

§ **Drink the potion and know that you are now a part of its power.**

If you already have someone special, then you could drink this potion together. If not, then drink the potion to cast the spell upon yourself and wait for him to notice! To enhance the power of this potion use it with The 'Look At Me' Spell (see page 53).

sleeping potion

What you need: one camomile herbal tea-bag, three drops of Cherry Plum Bach flower remedy, three drops of Rock Rose Bach flower remedy, two drops of Rescue Remedy, a little sugar or honey to sweeten.

Moon time: any – take last thing at night before bed.

 Steep the camomile tea-bag in boiling water for about five to ten minutes. Herbal teas need longer to infuse than ordinary tea-bags because they have a more delicate flavour.

 Add the flower remedies (Cherry Plum for soothing, Rock Rose for relaxing, and Rescue Remedy for calming and comforting) and then add a little sugar or honey to sweeten the potion.

 Take it to bed and sip it slowly as you mentally release all your worries and stress using the visualisation techniques you have developed in working through this book.

 When you have finished the potion, breathe deeply for a few minutes until you feel completely relaxed. You should now drop off to sleep quite easily.

To enhance this spell, put a few drops of lavender oil on your pillowcase, or use the old wives' trick of kissing your pillow and asking it for sweet dreams.

revitalising potion

What you need: one lemon and ginger herbal tea-bag, five drops of Oak Bach flower remedy, three drops of Walnut Bach flower remedy, a dash of lemon juice, a little sugar or honey to sweeten.

Moon time: any – drink whenever you feel lethargic or under the weather.

Steep the herbal tea-bag as usual for five to ten minutes. Add the flower remedies (Oak for strength and Walnut to ease the stress of puberty) and a dash of lemon juice (to uplift you). Now add a little sugar or honey to sweeten the potion.

Hold your power hand (the one you write with) over the potion and imagine you are sending pure white light into the drink. This light is energising and will add to the power of the potion.

Now drink the potion and prepare yourself to be magically uplifted.

Hearth Spells

To a witch, a home is much more than a roof to keep the rain off. It is a haven, a sanctuary where we can cast aside the stress and psychic dirt of the outside world. It is a place where we can be truly ourselves.

Our living spaces should be comforting, inviting places that give off a feeling of safety. They should be clean and free from any negative energy. This is not to say that your room must look like those in the pages of an interior design magazine – a room should feel lived in as well. But an untidy area can create chaos in our lives. Rather than feeling as if we've come into a sanctuary, we can feel instead as though we've entered a war zone. This may be especially true if you are a naturally untidy person and face constant rows about cleaning your room.

In this chapter we will be looking at ways in which you can magically enhance your own living space and help to create a happy home atmosphere using witchcraft.

One of the most important aspects of home life is a feeling of privacy, so we're going to begin right there, with a simple yet effective protection spell.

the bedroom guardian spell

To protect the privacy of your room, try invoking a guardian to keep watch at the door. Choose the type of guardian you want – this could be a vampire, a unicorn, an alien or a dragon. Anything goes as long as it's powerful, and possibly scary!

> **What you want:** to protect your space.
> **What you need:** your imagination, a figure or poster of your chosen guardian (optional).
> **Moon time:** full.

🌿 Sit in the middle of your room with your eyes closed and bring to mind an image of your guardian. When you can clearly see the guardian standing before you in your imagination, breathe into the image three times. This is known as breathing life into your spell. Watch as your guardian's eyes open and he or she asks for your instructions.

🌿 Now say the following words:

> *I name you ... (give the guardian a name).*
> *Your purpose is to protect my room and guard my door.*
> *Let no one invade my privacy or intrude on my private space.*
> *Go now and do as I bid.*

🌿 See your guardian walk to the door of your room and stand before it, guarding it from all unwelcome visitors.

To enhance this spell, remind your guardian daily of his or her job, and place the figure or poster near the door of your room. If you share a bedroom you can still invoke the guardian to protect your own half of the space.

simple cleansing

The new moon is the perfect time for cleansing rituals in which we are working to bring new, positive energies into our home. You should perform this cleansing ritual every new moon for the best results. If you cannot cleanse the whole house then stick to your own room, and the positive energy you create there will influence the rest of the house. It is also a good idea to do a cleansing ritual if there has been an argument between family members. A quick cleansing will dispel the negativity that has built up, and a reconciliation or apology will be much easier.

What you want: to cleanse an area of negative energies.

What you need: one white candle, a floral essential oil, water, salt, an incense cone, an apple, a knife, your pentacle.

Moon time: new.

🌿 Before you can do a magical cleansing, you must first perform a physical cleansing. Yep, that's right – to be a witch you've got to clean your room. Remember what I said about backing up your magic? Well, with cleansings the whole thing is reversed. First we clean physically with duster and vacuum cleaner, then we clean magically in the following way:

🌿 First open all the windows and allow the element of Air into the house.

🌿 Next, take the candle and anoint it with the floral essential oil. Place the candle in a sturdy holder and put it as close to the centre of the room as you possibly can, making sure it isn't going to get knocked over and keeping it away from anything flammable. Now light the wick and allow the candle to burn, filling the room with fragrance.

🌿 Now cut the apple in half along its equator line (horizontally) and you will notice that the seeds in the centre of the fruit form a five-pointed star or pentagram. This is why the apple is such a magical fruit and is known as the fruit of the Goddess in Wicca. (If you don't see a seed star in the centre of your apple, then you've cut it the wrong way. Get another and try again.) Place both halves of the apple on your pentacle to charge while you continue the cleansing.

🌿 Take a pinch of salt and add it to the water. Go around the room in a deosil (clockwise) direction and, using your fingers, flick droplets of water all around it saying:

> *By the Powers that Be,*
> *I cleanse this space.*

Repeat until you have cleansed the whole room.

※ **Pour the remainder of the salted water away to cleanse the drains.**

※ **Finally, pick up the apple halves and place them at opposite ends of the room. They will help to soak up any negativity that may be left. Leave them in place for 24 hours and then bury them in the garden.**

Do something quiet for the remainder of the day – perhaps read a book, listen to gentle music or get on with your homework. Allow the candle to burn for as long as you are in the room with it, then put it out before you leave.

happy home spell

One of the most magical ways to bring about a happy atmosphere in the home is to attune with the guardian spirit of the area on which your house is built. These guardians are known as household devas, and they can assist you in any magical workings that involve your home and family.

Household devas are generally neglected creatures, but magical people build up a relationship with these guardians to help us make our home life all that it can be. I have two white alabaster figures of goddess-type ladies, who stand at either side of my fireplace. To me, these figures represent the devas who watch over my house and garden. I place candles and crystals before them when I need their assistance with something.

> **What you want:** to create a happy atmosphere using the household devas.
> **What you need:** a small potted plant of

your choice, a rose quartz crystal, a supply of floral incense cones or sticks and the appropriate holder, a pretty pastel pink scarf (optional).

Moon time: waxing.

🌾 You can invoke your own household deva by setting up a small shrine somewhere in the home. If others in your family are not magically inclined, then set up the shrine in your room, but it must be a separate place and should not be a part of your working altar – the devas deserve their own space.

🌾 If you have one, spread the pink scarf over the surface you are going to use as a shrine. Put the plant in the middle, making sure that it is healthy – a dead plant would only insult your household guardian!

🌾 Next, take the rose quartz crystal – which stands for friendship and contentment and will honour the deva – and place it on one side of the plant. Put some burning incense at the other side. Say this invocation as the incense burns:

> *Household devas, gather here;*
> *I call you to this place.*
> *Put an end to pain and fear*
> *Within this time and space.*
> *Help to make this household strong,*
> *Its family full of love.*
> *This is where we all belong,*
> *Sharing joys from up above.*
> *As above, so below,*
> *Safety and happiness reign.*
> *As I will, it shall be so,*
> *Until I call on you again.*

For the best results, light the incense and repeat this invocation daily. You might like to copy out the invocation and keep it on your household deva shrine.

If you need extra help from the devas in a particular situation, simply go to the shrine, state your problem and ask for their support. Always perform the invocation first and take good care of the plant.

to resolve a family argument

What you want: to restore harmony in your family.

What you need: a piece of paper for every person involved in the dispute, a pen, a spoon, a jar of honey, an envelope.

Moon time: any – this is an emergency spell; perform it about one hour after the disagreement.

🌾 Take all the ingredients to your altar and on the slips of paper write the names of the people involved in the disagreement – one name to a slip.

🌾 Now comes the messy part. Using the spoon, spread a little honey on the slips of paper (symbolically to sweeten up the person named) and sandwich them together, making sure all the names and the honey face inwards.

🌾 When you have done this, put the sticky bundle in the envelope and seal it. Now say:

> *With this spell I stop harsh sound;*
> *I weave the magic round and round.*
> *Honey sweeten, honey stick,*
> *Family bonding now so thick,*
> *End the rows and end the spite,*
> *Magic make and hearts be light!*
> *So mote it be!*

🌾 Now take the envelope and either burn it and scatter the ashes, or bury it in the garden or local park.

cat return spell

I created this spell last year when my own cat, Pyewackett, had been gone for two days. It's very effective and I now use it whenever Pye has been gone for around 24 hours. It has always brought him back safely within the hour.

> **What you want:** to bring your cat home safely.
>
> **What you need:** your pentacle, a toy that belongs to your cat, a clean cat bowl, some cat treats.
>
> **Moon time:** any – perform whenever your cat has been gone for 24 hours or more

⚜ **Take all the items to your altar. Put the cat toy on the pentacle and pour a few cat treats into his bowl ready for when he returns. Save the rest of the cat treats as you'll be needing them later.**

⚜ **Now visualise your cat safe at home with you, and repeat the following charm nine times – one for each feline life – changing it to fit a female cat if necessary:**

> *Bring the cat I love and feed;*
> *Bring him home with all due speed.*
> *I accept that he will roam;*
> *Protect him on his journey home.*
> *A true companion I have found,*
> *So let my cat be homeward bound.*
> *Before the passing of one more day,*
> *Let my cat come home to stay.*
> *Bring him to me safe at last,*
> *This I ask of you, Queen Bast!*
> *So mote it be!*

⚜ **When your cat returns, give him the treats in the bowl. Take the rest of the treats outside and scatter them for any stray cats that may need them.**

- 🌿 Give thanks to Bast, the Egyptian cat goddess.
- 🌿 Now take the cat toy and have a game with your feline friend.

to protect a pet

This is a simple variation of the above spell.

> **What you want:** magically to protect a pet.
> **What you need:** a pentacle, a photo of your pet, sea salt.
> **Moon time:** full.

- 🌿 Place the photograph on the pentacle and surround the whole thing with a circle of salt.

- 🌿 At the same time focusing on the absolute safety and good health of your pet, chant the words:

    Protected Be!

- 🌿 Continue chanting until your focus has faded and then stop.

- 🌿 Leave the photo, pentacle and salt in place for 24 hours and then clear everything away.

- 🌿 Scatter a little of the salt under your pet's bed and throw the rest to the winds saying:

    Blessed Be!

to stop parents nagging

What you want: to stop a parent going on and on ...

What you need: a small strip of cardboard, black nail polish, a black pen, a small plastic box with a lid, water, access to a freezer.

Moon time: waning.

- On the strip of cardboard write down what you want to prevent. For example you might write, 'Stop Mum nagging about ...'

- Now take the black nail polish and paint over what you have just written so that no one can see it.

- Wait for the nail polish to dry, then put the slip of cardboard in the plastic box, fill it with water and put on the lid. Place the whole thing at the back of the freezer.

A word of warning – if this spell is allowed to defrost, the nagging may begin again. You've been warned!

a spell for peace and quiet

This is a very simple spell that works a treat if performed correctly. I have used it many times myself. The key is to be fully focused and strongly aware of your power as a witch.

> **What you want:** to stop noise and bring about a quiet time.
> **What you need:** a strong focus.
> **Moon time:** any – perform when you need it.

- **Using your power hand (the one you write with), direct the flat of your palm towards the direction of the disturbance – this could be the TV in the next room, the people next door, a barking dog and so on.**

- **Say very firmly as many times as you like:**

  Stop the noise!

  Remember that you are the witch, you are the one with the power, so make sure you speak with authority, but don't shout.

- **The noise will normally stop within 30 minutes or less, giving you the peace and quiet you need.**

This is an excellent way of shutting up those noisy neighbours who play loud music in the garden all summer long. Cast this spell and you will finally be able to get the peace you need to revise for your exams.

Hearth Spells

healing heart spell

This spell will help you to deal with the pain of loss if someone you love has died or your parents have separated. It will also help you to grow close to new step-parents, step-sisters and step-brothers.

> **What you want:** to remain or become close to those that you name.
> **What you need:** pink paper, scissors, a red pen, a glue stick, rose petals, a pink envelope.
> **Moon time:** full.

※ **Begin by cutting a love heart out of the pink paper. It should be able to fit into the envelope when folded in half, so don't make it too big. Fold the heart in half.**

※ **On one side write your own name; on the other side write the name of the person who has gone from your life, or the names of the people who have come into your life and who you would like to feel close to. Now unfold the heart and fold it again the other way, making the two names touch one another.**

※ **Using the glue stick, glue the edges of the heart together, thus sealing the bond.**

※ **Now place the heart in the envelope and add the rose petals for love. Seal the envelope and keep it somewhere safe, such as your altar, and remember that time is a universal heal-all. The spell is done.**

to protect the home

What you want: to keep your home safe.
What you need: your wand.
Moon time: full.

- Go around the whole house drawing pentagrams on all the windows and doors with your wand.

- Next, go outside and draw a circle around your entire home. If this isn't possible, simply visualise the circle. Visualise your home now completely protected from all harm, at the same time stating that this is so.

- Repeat this spell regularly to maintain the magic.

Pentagrams are the oldest and strongest form of magical protection, and that is what is used in this spell. You can also adapt it to protect your bicycle, the family car and so on. This is a protection spell without limits.

Social Spells

In this chapter we will be looking at a series of spells centred around friendships and social occasions.

sorry spell

What you want: to make apologising a little easier.

What you need: a pen and paper, matches, a heatproof bowl.

Moon time: new – or whenever needed.

〰 **On the piece of paper copy out the following charm:**

I call on powers from up above
In perfect trust and perfect love.
Sorry I am and will be too.
Sorry is the word I'll say to you.
I'll try my best to make us friends.
With this spell our disagreement ends.
Apologise I know I must,
In perfect love and perfect trust.
So mote it be!

〰 **After writing out the charm, repeat it three times aloud.**

〰 **Then fold the paper and burn it carefully in the heatproof bowl.**

〰 **Scatter the ashes in the garden as soon as they have cooled.**

〰 **Make your apology as soon as you can.**

to improve communications

Citrine is a member of the quartz family and is well known among witches for its ability to improve communications.

> **What you want:** to open lines of communication with someone.
> **What you need:** a citrine crystal, your chalice, spring water.
> **Moon time:** full or waxing.

Put the citrine crystal into the chalice and then fill the chalice with pure spring water.

Now place the chalice in direct sunlight for at least a couple of hours – longer if you can.

Once the water has been fully charged by the crystal and sunlight, it is known as a crystal essence potion.

Carefully remove the citrine from the potion and dry it with a soft cloth or leave it to dry in the sun. Now drink the potion, visualising yourself communicating easily with the particular person you have in mind.

Next, give the citrine to this person as a gift, so connecting them with your spell.

Communication should now become much easier, but if things have been very difficult don't expect too much at first. True communication comes only with trust, and trust takes time to build. This spell will serve to get the ball rolling.

to stop copy-cats

It can be really annoying when someone copies everything you do – your clothes, your hair styles, the things you buy and so on. While on one level it is very flattering that this person admires you so much that they want to be just like you and own everything you own, at the same time it can leave you feeling stripped of your individuality. So use this little spell to steer them in their own direction.

> **What you want:** to dissuade a person from copying you.
> **What you need:** a piece of card, a piece of paper, 1 metre/1 yard of black ribbon, sticky tape, a black pen.
> **Moon time:** waning.

᛭ **Copy the following charm on to a piece of paper:**

> *Copy-cat! Stop that!*
> *To take my idea, speaks of fear.*
> *Be yourself; be who you are,*
> *Or else you'll never get too far.*
> *I am me, you are you;*
> *From yourself take your cue!*
> *You are you, I am me;*
> *So ends this game – so mote it be!*

᛭ **Now write the name of the copy-cat in black pen on the piece of card.**

᛭ **Fold the paper, with the charm written on it, around the card.**

᛭ **Now say the charm aloud three times, and as you do so, bind the card and paper together by wrapping the black ribbon around them.**

᛭ **Secure the end of the ribbon with sticky tape, and carry the spell in your school bag, pencil case or pocket.**

Repeat the spell once a month if necessary.

gag the gossip spell

This spell will effectively silence anyone who is gossiping about you.

What you want: to stop gossip.
What you need: modelling clay or dough, a piece of black ribbon, an inscribing tool, your pentacle.
Moon time: waning.

Take the clay or dough and create a magical poppet by fashioning it into a basic human shape – similar to a gingerbread man.

Using the inscribing tool, carve the name of the gossip on the tummy of the poppet and make a small line to represent a mouth.

Now tie the black ribbon around the mouth and head of the poppet, symbolically gagging the culprit.

Place the poppet on top of your pentacle and put the whole thing in a dark drawer.

When the gossip has stopped, take the poppet, without removing the gag, and bury it in the earth.

The spell is complete.

for a great birthday

What you want: to ensure you have an extra-special day.

What you need: florists' oasis, seven birthday candles and holders in your favourite colour or colours, matches.

Moon time: any – perform just before your birthday.

- Seven days before your birthday take all the items to your altar to begin the spell.

- Place the candle holders in the oasis so that they form a circle.

- Pick up the first birthday candle and hold it in your hands. Strongly visualise all that you hope this coming birthday will bring. Continue as long as you remain totally focused.

- Now set the candle in one of the holders and light it. Meditate on the flame as you once again concentrate on all your birthday hopes. Keep watching the candle until it burns itself out.

- Repeat this process every day until all the candles are gone.

- On the day after your birthday, remove and clean the candle holders and put them away for next year. Throw away the oasis or use it for arranging flowers.

- Finally, put an offering of nuts and seeds outside for the wildlife as a way of giving thanks for the great birthday you have had.

to strengthen friendship

This is a spell that you can do with a friend or by yourself.

What you want: to make a friendship stronger.
What you need: three narrow ribbons (about 15 cm/6 in long) in your friend's favourite colours, lavender essential oil, your pentacle.
Moon time: waxing.

- **Take the three different coloured ribbons (they can also be different shades of the same colour) and tie a knot close to one end.**
- **Now get a friend to hold that end or secure it in some other way, and begin to plait the ribbons. As you do so, remember all the good times you and your friend have shared and think about a bright and happy friendship that lasts through thick and thin.**
- **When you have neatly plaited all the ribbons together, secure the end with a knot and place it on your pentacle to charge for three days.**
- **After this time, sprinkle the friendship bracelet with a few drops of lavender oil and then give it to your friend to wear around her wrist.**

This spell can be adapted to create your own set of magical cords. Simply use longer pieces of ribbon and charge them to your magical purpose, for example sweet dreams. Make sure you choose the appropriate colour and oil for your goal (see pages 25–6).

for a great party or sleep-over

This is a simple spell that will give any party a buzz.

What you want: to make a friendly gathering go with a swing.

What you need: an empty spritzer bottle, spring water, five drops of ylang-ylang essential oil, five drops of geranium essential oil, six to eight tea-lights and holders.

Moon time: full – a great night for a gathering!

- First cast a Circle around the whole room, making sure your visualisation is strong and clear.

- Next mix together the essential oils and spring water and pour the mixture into the spritzer bottle. Give it a good shake.

- Go around the house spraying the potion, imagining sunlight and rainbows filling your home as you do so.

- Finally, place the tea-lights in holders and position them in the main room of the party, so that they form a kind of inner circle around the edge of the room.

- Just before your guests begin to arrive, light the candles and wish for a great party.

for a fun weekend

What you want: to make sure you have a fabulous weekend.

What you need: a skipping rope or a ball.

Moon time: any – perform on a Friday evening.

- For this spell you will need to learn the words of the charm by heart.

- When you have done so, take the skipping rope or ball outside and skip out the charm, chanting it aloud, or bounce the ball on the ground or against a wall. The movement of your body will help to get things moving:

> *Friday's my day – school is out!*
> *Set me free and let me out!*
> *Saturday, Sunday,*
> *Weekend fun day,*
> *Joy is what it's all about!*

- Continue until you are tired, and then look forward to a great weekend.

It's the movement and the chanting that move the magic, so you can use this spell with any repetitive physical activity.

Social Spells

fashion swap spell

If you would like to borrow a friend's outfit for a special occasion, then try this spell.

> **What you want:** to borrow a friend's outfit.
> **What you need:** silver glitter, a fashion doll such as Barbie (or a poppet), clothes to fit the doll.
> **Moon time:** full.

- First dress the doll in her best clothes. She now represents your friend and the outfit you would like to borrow.

- Pour a little of the silver glitter into your hand, and focus on your friend smiling as she lends you the outfit. Keep this up for as long as you can.

- Then blow the newly charged glitter over the fashion doll.

- The spell is complete.

To enhance the spell, you might like to offer one of your outfits to your friend in a temporary swap. This will complete the exchange of energy.

to get back something you've lent

You can use this spell to draw back anything you have lent to a friend. This could be an outfit, make-up, CDs, a book and so on. (A word of warning here – you should never lend your spell books to people as they are considered to be magical tools. You wouldn't lend your altar set-up to someone, and magical books are no different. By all means copy out and share spells, but keep the books to yourself.) On with the spell ...

> **What you want:** to get back an object
> you have lent to someone.
> **What you need:** a yo-yo.
> **Moon time:** waxing.

Take the yo-yo and begin to play it up and down as you repeat this spell:

> *What is mine returns to me,*
> *By the power of three times three.*
> *What is mine returns to me.*
> *This is my will. So mote it be!*

Continue for as long as you remain focused, and repeat daily until your belongings are returned.

social spells

to attract new friends

What you want: to meet and draw to you new friends.
What you need: nothing.
Moon time: waxing.

To draw new friends into your life repeat these words as many times as you can while remaining focused:

Like pebbles on a beach,
New friends I will reach.
Like soft grains of sand
Between sea and land,
New friends come to me,
Like waves on the sea.
Endlessly driven,
Ceaselessly given.
Companions I need,
So I'm planting the seed.
As the moon shines above,
Friendship is love.
I give as I take,
So new friends I make.
Endlessly driven,
Ceaselessly given.
Like waves on the sea,
New friends come to me.

If you can, say these words on a beach or near a source of water – the bath will do just fine.

to resist pressure from friends

Sometimes your friends can try to make you do things you don't really want to do, from smoking a cigarette or trying drugs to having a boyfriend or having sex before you are actually ready. This is known as peer pressure and most of us have experienced it at some time or other. Use this spell to guard against this negative influence and make you strong enough in yourself to do what you want to do.

> **What you want:** to be able to resist the unwanted influence of friends.
> **What you need:** your memory, a strong will!
> **Moon time:** any – use when you need.

Memorise this spell and say it three times in your head whenever you feel you are being pressured:

> *My life is my own.*
> *May this influence be gone!*
> *I must do as I choose,*
> *And if your friendship I lose,*
> *Then you are no true friend,*
> *And this is the end.*
> *But if your friendship remains,*
> *Then a true friend I've gained.*
> *My life is my own.*
> *Influence be gone!*

Remember that the most powerful magic is always to be true to yourself. The strongest people don't just follow the crowd, they create their own path through life.

social spells

How to Get What You Want

In this chapter you will find a variety of spells that will help you to take charge of your life and generally feel more in control.

to bring something you want

What you want: to gain your desires.
What you need: a bag of alphabet sweets, your pentacle.
Moon time: full.

☽ Using the alphabet sweets spell out exactly what it is you want – a stereo, a holiday, a new phone and so on – but remember that magic will only bring you what you want if you also genuinely need it.

☽ Now place the words you have made on your pentacle and allow them to charge overnight.

☽ The following morning, before you do anything else, eat the sweets and say:

It comes to me, so mote it be!

☽ The spell is complete.

to encourage change

The cauldron is the witch's tool of transformation. In nature the butterfly is symbolic of great change, having once been a caterpillar. In this spell we will be using both these symbols.

> **What you want:** to make a positive change in your life.
>
> **What you need:** a sheet of paper, coloured crayons or felt tip pens, a pen, a cauldron, food colouring, three dried bay leaves, three floating candles, an envelope.
>
> **Moon time:** waxing.

֎ First draw and cut out the shape of a butterfly – it should be just big enough to go into the envelope when folded in half. Now use the coloured crayons or felt tip pens to decorate the butterfly and make it beautiful.

֎ On the back on the butterfly write down the change you would like to make. Narrow this change down to a single word, or maybe two words, and write this down on each of the dried bay leaves.

֎ Next, fill your cauldron with water. Add a few drops of food colouring, the colour of which should match your magical goal. Now carefully float the three bay leaves and the floating candles on the surface of the water.

֎ Light the candles and allow them to burn down. You will need to remain in the circle as this takes place, so bring a book or your homework to your magical place.

֎ Once the candles have burnt out, remove the leaves and fold them into the paper butterfly, saying three times:

> *Butterfly wings – transform these things!*

- Now put the butterfly and the leaves into the envelope and seal it.

- When the change you require has taken place, burn the envelope and its contents, giving thanks that your magic has worked.

to make a wish come true

What you want: to make your wishes reality.
What you need: a bottle of magic bubbles.
Moon time: from new to full.

- Take the bottle of bubbles outside and visualise your magical goal for a few minutes.

- Now begin to blow bubbles. As you do so, imagine that you are breathing life and magic into your wish. This wish is inside every bubble that you have blown, and the air carries it out into the universe. As each bubble bursts, your wish is released and is brought one step closer to manifestation.

- Continue for as long as your focus remains clear.

This is a lovely spell as it gets you outside and demonstrates how natural energies (the wind) combine with our own energies (breath) to make magic happen.

to help you give up smoking

Before you begin this spell you will need to have made (but not stuffed) a fabric poppet. This should be a simple human shape (like a gingerbread man), and you should leave a hole at the top of the head for stuffing.

> **What you want:** to kick the habit.
> **What you need:** cigarettes, a fabric poppet, shredded paper.
> **Moon time:** waning.

۞ **Charge your cigarettes and the poppet on your pentacle for three hours before beginning. During this time you may have your very last cigarette. Use it as an instrument of farewell and say goodbye to your addiction.**

۞ **Now go back to your altar and take up the poppet. Begin to stuff it with shredded paper – the type sold in pet shops is ideal.**

۞ **When the poppet is half full, take the cigarettes and crumble them into the doll. Don't think of it as wasted cigarettes, think of it as clean, pink lungs and a long and healthy life.**

۞ **After putting all the cigarettes into the poppet, finish stuffing it with shredded paper.**

۞ **Now stitch up the rest of the head and dispose of the poppet by floating it away on a living body of water such as a brook or a stream. Alternatively, you could burn or bury the poppet. Dispose of it as soon as you have completed the spell.**

Repeat this process as often as you feel you need to. Giving up smoking won't be easy (nothing worth doing ever is) and you will need lots of willpower. Use the Craft to help you. You can enhance this spell by using it in combination with the To Encourage Change spell (see pages 94–5).

to change your luck

This is a spell of two halves. In the first half of the spell we work to banish any bad luck that may be hanging around, while the second half of the spell attracts good luck and fortune.

> **What you want:** to attract a run of good luck and banish bad luck.
> **What you need:** a black candle, a small strip of paper, black thread, a black pen, a good luck charm, your pentacle, a sweet-smelling essential oil of your choice.
> **Moon time:** full.

ဒ **To begin with, hold the black candle in your hands and allow all the bad luck that you have experienced to be absorbed by the wax.**

ဒ **Now write the following on the slip of paper:**

> *An end to luck that's black as black;*
> *May good fortune replace the lack.*

ဒ **Wrap the paper around the base of the candle, words facing inwards, and secure it with the black thread. Now place the candle in a sturdy holder and take the whole thing and put it in the bath, well away from anything flammable.**

ဒ **Light the wick and allow the candle to burn away your bad luck. The spell paper will catch fire as the candle burns, which is why it should be put somewhere extra safe – in this case the bath.**

Now for the second half of the spell.

ဒ **To attract good luck you should find or buy yourself a lucky charm – one that is gentle on nature, so no rabbit's feet. A four-leaf clover necklace would be ideal, or perhaps a pentagram necklace or Celtic talisman.**

- ⟨ Put the item on your pentagram to charge for a while and add a couple of drops of essential oil.

- ⟨ Once you feel that your talisman is fully charged, take it and carry it with you always.

for a good night's sleep

What you want: to enjoy a restful, undisturbed night of sleep.
What you need: a pretty bowl, lavender oil, dried lavender heads.
Moon time: full.

- ⟨ Take all the items to your altar and place them there to charge on your pentacle for three hours before working the spell.

- ⟨ Then carefully empty the dried lavender heads into the bowl. The bowl should be attractive and, if possible, match the decor of your room.

- ⟨ Next, add five drops of lavender oil to the dried flowers and say this charm five times:

  > *With this spell, sleep be deep.*
  > *I close my eyes, no worries keep.*
  > *Black as the night,*
  > *As the sun fades from sight.*
  > *As I cast this spell, in dreams I dwell.*
  > *So mote it be!*

- ⟨ Now place the bowl of flowers by your bedside and put a few drops of lavender oil on to your pillow.

- ⟨ Finally, just before getting into bed, rub a drop or two of lavender oil on to your wrists and temples. Then close your eyes and enjoy a full night's restful sleep.

to invoke a shopping guru

This spell is a variation of the Bedroom Guardian Spell on pages 69–70. Here we will work to invoke a thought form in the shape of a shopping guru. First think of someone who knows a lot about what you want to shop for. This doesn't have to be a real person, you can create someone specifically for this spell. In fact, you'll probably get much better results if you design your own guru. For instance, if you are shopping for clothes, design a supermodel-type guru, or if you are shopping for books, design a librarian-type guru. Your guru should be in complete harmony with your shopping goal.

> **What you want:** to create your own personal shopping guru.
> **What you need:** your imagination.
> **Moon time:** full.

- Once you have decided what type of guru you would like, picture them in your mind. When you can 'see' them standing before you, breathe into them three times and ask them to go shopping with you. Tell them exactly what you want and how much money you have. Now ask them to steer you towards a great bargain. You may find yourself visiting shops you've never been in before.

- Once you have found the item you wanted and have returned home with it, release your shopping guru by saying:

> *Thank you for your help. I now release you. Please come again when I have need of you.*

Know that you can call on this particular guru whenever you like, or you can create more for different shopping tasks. Always remember to give thanks and to release the magical energy of the thought form when you have finished.

for sweet dreams

Scented herb pillows have long been used by magical people to bring about sweet dreams and psychic visions. Although herb pillows can be bought, they can easily be made at home for a fraction of the price.

> **What you want:** to enjoy pleasant and psychic dreams.
>
> **What you need:** a piece of fabric large enough to make a small pillow, dried lavender flowers, dried camomile flowers, dried mugwort, lace and ribbons to trim (optional), needle and thread.
>
> **Moon time:** full.

❧ **First sew your fabric into a basic pillow shape, leaving one end open for stuffing. The type of fabric you use is your choice, but both felt and velvet are easily sewn and pleasant to lie on. Also bear in mind that an open fabric such as lace will allow the dried flowers to spill out.**

❧ **Next take equal parts of dried lavender (for sleep), camomile (for relaxation) and mugwort (for psychic visions) and stuff the pillow. How much of the dried flower mixture you need depends entirely on the size of your pillow.**

❧ **Once the pillow is nicely stuffed, sew up the remaining side and trim it with lace and ribbons.**

❧ **Place the magical pillow on your bed, on top of your ordinary pillow, and look forward to meaningful dreams.**

to find something you've lost, or for psychic development

Witches often use a form of scrying (psychic searching or future-gazing) called pendulum dowsing. We use this technique to answer yes/no questions or to find something that is lost. You will need some kind of pendulum. This could be one bought from a New Age store, or you could use a necklace and pendant, or a ring suspended from a chain. You could also tie a key to a length of ribbon and use that as a pendulum. Before I bought my crystal pendulum, I used a bead necklace that has a collection of sea shells hung from the end. Be creative and use whatever you have to hand.

To begin with you will need to discover how the pendulum moves for you. This varies from witch to witch and from pendulum to pendulum. There's no right or wrong way for the pendulum to move. For me, the pendulum moves back and forth to indicate 'yes' and widdershins to indicate 'no'.

To find out the movement of your pendulum, ask it a question to which you know the answer is 'yes' and record the way it moves. Then ask a question to which you know the answer is 'no' and note the change in direction.

What you want: to locate a lost object, or to improve your psychic abilities.
What you need: some form of pendulum, a map (optional).
Moon time: new to full.

- **Go from room to room, or hold the pendulum over a map, and say:**

  The object I've lost is here?

- **Watch to see the way the pendulum reacts. Remember to hold the chain of the pendulum loosely but firmly, allowing the pendulum to swing any way it will. Do not try to control its movements.**

This magical technique is a great way of improving your psychic ability. Get a friend to hide an object and use your pendulum to find it. Take turns. Begin in a single room and then, as you get better at it, move a little further afield.

safe travel spell

What you want: to travel safely.
What you need: a tiger's eye crystal, your pentacle, two pieces of paper, a pen.
Moon time: waxing.

- Place the crystal on the pentacle over a piece of paper on which you have written the words 'safe travel'. The crystal is now being empowered to your magical purpose.

- On the second piece of paper write the following:

  From north to south, from south to
  *   north,*
  Guard me as I go back and forth.

- Beneath these words draw two arrows facing in opposite directions.

- Now repeat the charm as many times as you like, all the time focusing on safe travel.

- Just before your journey, place the crystal and the two slips of paper in your luggage or in your purse. Keep them safe.

- On your safe return home, rip up the papers and scatter them to the winds, giving thanks. Rinse the crystal underneath the cold tap to cleanse it.

faerie magic

The following spells all fall into the category of faerie magic. Yes, witches do believe in faeries and work with them regularly! Here you will learn how to work your own faerie spells.

to make things grow

Most herbs can be grown indoors on a sunny window sill, and you can then provide your own spell ingredients. Lavender is great in the bedroom as it induces sleep. Never plant anything after the full moon, as the natural energy is all wrong. Do your planting only during the cycle of new to full moon.

> **What you want:** successfully to grow plants inside the house or in the garden.
> **What you need:** your chosen herbs or plants, an image of a faerie (one that can be left among your plants), a rose quartz crystal, green water from your rainbow waters range (see pages 58–9).
> **Moon time:** new to full.

ζ **Carefully arrange your chosen plants in the garden, or in pretty pots, or in a window-box.**

ζ **Place your faerie figure and rose quartz crystal among the plants and hold your hands over the whole thing. Repeat this spell three times:**

> *By faerie magic these plants grow,*
> *As above, so below.*
> *By the power between the Earth and skies,*
> *I command these plants to grow and thrive,*
> *Their beauty here for all to see.*
> *This is my will, so mote it be!*

ζ **Now carefully tend your plants and water them with magically empowered green water.**

weather witching

Weather witching, as it is known, can be fun, but you should always work with nature, not against her. Not only does this add to your chances of success, but it also shows a wise witch at work. If your weather spells don't work, then just try again another day and remember that sometimes nature knows best. Also bear in mind that your snowy day may cause problems for someone else, so always cast with harm to none.

spell for rain

What you want: to bring the rain.
What you need: your cauldron – filled with water, your wand.
Moon time: any – use when you need.

- Fill your cauldron with water and take it outside along with your wand. You may get wet during this spell, so be prepared!

- Hold your cauldron in the crook of one arm, or with one hand if it is small enough. Then, with your power hand, use your wand to stir the water in a deosil (clockwise) direction. Stir faster and faster until the water slops and splashes, and chant:

    Like to like, gain to gain,
    Bring the clouds, make it rain!

- Continue chanting until the water is slopping all around the cauldron and the power has been raised.

- Then, at the final chant, throw all the water up into the air.

The magic is now in progress. I have used this spell quite a few times and generally find that it takes effect in a few hours.

sunny days spell

What you want: to bring a sunny day.
What you need: a torch, a round mirror.
Moon time: any – use when you need.

- Go outside and hold up the round mirror. Now shine the torch into the mirror to make it represent the sun.

- Repeat this chant nine times:

  Wind, chase the clouds away;
  Bring about a sunny day.
  Mirror high and torch below,
  Call out the sun's fiery glow.
  With the help of the fey,
  I bring about a sunny day!

- After the chant put your tools away and leave out a bowl of milk for the wildlife and the fey (another term for faeries). This completes the exchange of energy.

spell for snow

This spell falls on tricky ground. While snow is a lot of fun for young people, too much snow can be disruptive and dangerous, especially for the elderly, so you must cast this spell with harm to none and be very sensible. You should work it only on cold winter days, to be in harmony with nature.

What you want: to bring snow in winter.
What you need: rock salt, winter clothes.
Moon time: any – cast in winter.

- **Dress as though the snow is already here, in scarf and gloves, etc.**

- **Now go outside, taking the rock salt with you. If you don't have rock salt, any white powder will do. As a child I used to play 'snow and rain' games with talcum powder and an old washing-up liquid bottle filled with water.**

- **Scatter the rock salt around your path, drive or yard – salt is harmful to grass and plants so avoid these.**

- **As you do so, say:**

    Round, round, round I go;
    As I go, I make it snow!

- **Continue until paved areas have a light dusting of 'snow'. Then wait for your spell to work.**

Spells for Love

Love spells are probably the most popular in the Craft, followed closely by spells to attract money. Magic worked for love carries its own set of responsibilities – the most important being that you cannot direct a love spell towards a specific person. This goes back to the 'bending will' issue we talked about on page 11. A love spell that is directed towards a specific person is considered unethical, and true witches always observe ethics. Does this mean that you cannot work magic to attract someone? Of course not, but the spell should always be cast around yourself and with your ideal in mind. If the one you like is right for you, the magic will bring him to you. If not, the magic will bring the one who is right for you. The following spells all work to attract the one who is right for you at this particular time. Keep your options open and visualise your ideal boyfriend. If you break the rules and name a particular person, then you'll have to suffer the consequences – which may not be what you expected. You've been warned!

to warm a cold heart

What you want: to warm the heart of one you love.
What you need: a chalice, warm water, an ice cube, an inscribing tool.
Moon time: full.

\\\ **Fill your chalice with warm water.**

\\\ **Take an ice cube fresh from the freezer and inscribe a heart on to it. Inside the heart, inscribe your loved one's initials.**

- ⦙ Pop the ice cube into the warm water and set your chalice on the altar. Wait for the ice cube to melt, so melting the heart.

- ⦙ Once the ice has melted completely, drink the water to complete the spell. The person's attitude towards you should change.

to make someone come to you

What you want: to attract your ideal partner.
What you need: a reel of red cotton, an empty cotton reel.
Moon time: waxing.

- ⦙ Take both cotton reels to your altar and sit for a time thinking of all that you want in a boyfriend. Visualise your ideal, and as you do so, begin to wrap the red cotton around the empty reel, effectively transferring the thread from one reel to the other.

- ⦙ While you are doing this, you should chant the following charm, continuing throughout the duration of the spell:

> *Power of the witches rise;*
> *Send my words across the skies.*
> *I call you to me;*
> *Hear my plea.*
> *I weave, I spin,*
> *I reel you in.*

- ⦙ Once you have transferred all the cotton, put both reels in a safe place and wait for the spell to work.

to bring a partner back

If you have had a disagreement with your boyfriend, or a separation, this spell can be worked to reunite the two of you. However, it will only be effective if your love wants to return to you, in which case it will serve to give him the courage he needs to approach you.

> **What you want:** to bring back a lost love, if they wish to return.
> **What you need:** red paper, a pen, red ribbon.
> **Moon time:** full.

〰️ **Cut a love heart from the red paper and visualise the two of you in a happy time you shared together.**

〰️ **Now write this charm on the heart:**

> *Before the moon is full six times more,*
> *You will be knocking on my door!*

〰️ **Now roll the paper heart into a scroll and tie it with the red ribbon. Put it somewhere safe.**

If your love returns to you within six months, then burn or bury the spell. If he doesn't then it is not meant to be – float the spell away on a living body of water and ask for emotional healing.

to encourage someone to call you

What you want: to persuade a person to ring you.

What you need: a slip of paper, a pen, a citrine crystal, a rose quartz crystal, lavender essential oil, your pentacle.

Moon time: any – use when you need it.

\\\ **Write your phone number on the slip of paper. Drop a few drops of lavender oil on to the paper, then fold it in half.**

\\\ **Now put it on your pentacle and place the citrine (for communication) and rose quartz (for love and friendship) on top.**

\\\ **Leave them to charge for about an hour. Then put the crystals by your phone and either keep the paper with your phone number close by you, or be really cheeky and give it to him!**

You should receive a call within 24 hours.

\\\

to meet someone nice

This spell uses the power of the evening star, also known as the planet Venus. It is the first star to appear in the sky, usually around sunset.

> **What you want:** magically to improve your chances of meeting someone nice.
> **What you need:** a spell written by yourself, an envelope.
> **Moon time:** full.

\\\ First write your own spell, calling on Venus and asking her to bring someone really nice into your life. Include all the things that you want in a boyfriend and try to make the spell rhyme. Spend time over this and make sure that your spell will harm none.

\\\ Once you have written your spell, go outside at sunset and look for Venus.

\\\ Repeat your spell to this star three times and keep the spell paper in a sealed envelope on your altar.

\\\ Your spell will manifest in due course.

to find out if someone likes you

For this spell you will need to make a set of divination stones. Divination is the art of 'seeing', or fortune-telling. Here we are going to use this ancient art to find out if the one you dream of likes you too.

> **What you want:** to find out whether the person you like, likes you too.
>
> **What you need:** six flat pebbles or coloured glass nuggets, silver nail polish, a small pouch or purse, a purple candle (optional), sunflower oil (optional), dried mugwort (optional).
>
> **Moon time:** full.

\\\ Take the pebbles or glass nuggets and on three of them paint the word 'yes' using the silver nail polish. On the other three paint the word 'no'.

\\\ Wait until the nail polish has dried completely, then repeat the process on the other side of the pebbles, making sure you paint 'yes' on the 'yes' stones and 'no' on the 'no' stones! Once again, leave the pebbles to dry and then put them in the pouch.

\\\ When you are ready to use the stones, rub a little sunflower oil on to the purple candle and then roll it into a little dried mugwort. Mugwort is very well known amongst witches for inducing visions, and so it's perfect for fortune-telling spells.

\\\ Now shake the pouch and concentrate on the face of the one you admire. Dip your hand in the pouch and pull out a pebble. You now have your answer.

You can use this spell for absolutely any question that has a yes/no answer. You can also turn it into a fun game and take turns with your friends!

to cool down a situation

What you want: to defuse a situation that has become too intense or heavy.
What you need: a slip of paper, a pen, a small plastic box with a lid, water.
Moon time: waning – or cast whenever you feel out of your depth.

\\\ **On the slip of paper, write down briefly the situation that is bothering you.**

\\\ **Leave this paper on your altar for three hours and then put it in the plastic tub.**

\\\ **Fill the tub with water and put the lid on.**

\\\ **Put the whole thing in the freezer and leave it there for as long as possible.**

to prevent someone taking your partner

What you want: to prevent a person coming between you and your boyfriend.
What you need: a matchbox, a slip of paper, a pen, black thread, a black ribbon.
Moon time: waning.

\\\ **Write the name of your rival on the slip of paper.**

\\\ **Visualise this person finding her own boyfriend and leaving yours alone.**

\\\ **Now roll up the slip of paper so that it forms a little scroll. Secure it with black thread and put it in the matchbox.**

\\\ **Finally, tie the whole thing with black ribbon and bury it in the earth, somewhere away from your home.**

to nurture a new relationship

What you want: to encourage a new love to blossom and grow.
What you need: a plant, a plant pot, a red ribbon.
Moon time: new.

\\\ Pick a plant that can be grown indoors and one that you would like to have in your room. Lavender is a good plant to choose, or perhaps a miniature rose tree to symbolise love.

\\\ Place the plant carefully in your chosen pot and take it to your altar.

\\\ Hold your hands over it and say the following words:

I name this plant for my love
As this plant flourishes and grows,
so does our relationship.

\\\ Now tie the red ribbon around the plant pot and tend the plant carefully.

\\\ You can leave the plant on your altar as a decoration or you can put it in a sunny window.

to find out if he's the one

Work this spell on the night of the full moon as this is the best time for fortune-telling and divination of any kind.

> **What you want:** to see if a boyfriend is your true love.
> **What you need:** a pendulum, a photo of your boyfriend, your pentacle.
> **Moon time:** full.

\\\ **Place the photo of your boyfriend on the pentacle. If you do not have a photograph, then you can write his full name on a piece of paper and use that instead.**

\\\ **Now take up your pendulum and hold it steadily over the photo.**

\\\ **Say the following charm and note the way the pendulum moves to find your answer:**

> *Is he for me, does he like me?*
> *Give me now an answer.*
> *Does he love me, love me truly?*
> *Tell me now the answer.*

to stop someone calling you

This is a simple spell that will help to dissolve a person's need to call you. For safety, cast the spell in the kitchen sink.

> **What you want:** to prevent a person phoning you.
>
> **What you need:** the person's phone number, a piece of paper, salt, garlic powder, a tea-light, an ashtray.
>
> **Moon time:** waning – or use when you need.

\\\ **Write the person's phone number on the slip of paper.**

\\\ **In the centre of this paper place a pinch of salt (for cleansing) and a pinch of garlic powder (for banishing) and carefully fold up the paper.**

\\\ **Now light the tea-light, then light the paper from the flame of the candle and let it burn in the ash-tray. Put the tea-light in a suitable holder and allow it to burn for as long as you are in the room with it.**

The calls should now stop.

\\\

to make someone back off

What you want: magically to banish someone and make them leave you alone.

What you need: the person's name, a slip of paper, a black balloon, a pin, some of the person's hair (optional).

Moon time: dark.

\\\ Write the person's name on the slip of paper.

\\\ Roll up the paper and put it into the balloon through the neck. If you have a hair clipping, roll this into the paper first.

\\\ Next, blow up the balloon and tie a knot in the neck. Now hold the balloon and repeat these words:

Banished, banished, banished be!

\\\ As you do so, clearly visualise your enemy leaving you alone and staying right away from you.

\\\ Once you have done this, take the balloon outside and pop it with the pin. Put the whole thing in the bin and close the lid firmly. It is done.

to make breaking up easier

What you want: to ease the pain of making a break.

What you need: a balloon of your favourite colour, a ribbon of your favourite colour, note paper, a pen, a windy day.

Moon time: waning.

- Take the note paper and briefly write down your sad feelings and why you need to break up the relationship.

- Roll this paper up as tightly and as small as you can and put it into the balloon through the neck.

- Now blow up the balloon, visualising a pain-free break-up and an easy goodbye. Tie a knot in the neck of the balloon and tie the ribbon around it.

- Go outside on a windy day and walk to the top of a nearby hill.

- Say a final goodbye and let the balloon go. As it blows away it takes all your troubles with it. You will now find it easier to say goodbye and move on with your own life.

Spells for School and Work

Sometimes school can be a real drag, with projects and homework to produce on demand, and maybe even the school bully on your back. The spells in this chapter will provide magical answers for most of these problems. By using some of these spells you can make your school life run much more smoothly. We will also be looking at magical job hunting so that you can find the Saturday job that's right for you.

bind the bully

What you want: to stop someone from bullying you.

What you need: a small strip of stiff card, black nail polish, 1 metre/1 yard of black ribbon, a black marker pen, black electrical tape.

Moon time: dark.

- Take the piece of card and on it write the name of the bully in black marker pen.

- Next, paint over the surface of the card using the black nail polish, effectively blacking out the bully's name so that you can no longer see it. Allow the nail polish to dry.

꧁ **Then take the black ribbon and wrap it around the card, repeating the following chant:**

> *I bind the bully from doing harm,*
> *I bind the bully and embrace the calm.*

꧁ **Continue to chant until all the ribbon has been tightly bound around the card, then fix the end of the ribbon in place with a piece of black electrical tape.**

꧁ **Bury the whole thing at the bottom of the garden or in the soil of a potted plant.**

If bullying gets out of hand, always talk to your parents, a teacher or another responsible adult about it. Don't suffer in silence.

to get on with a teacher

We all know that there are some teachers we like – and some we don't.

> **What you want:** to get on with a teacher who's been picking on you.
> **What you need:** biscuits you have baked yourself.
> **Moon time:** full.

꧁ **Begin by baking the biscuits. You can do this at home or in your cookery class. If you are worried about your cooking skills, stick to something simple. Shortbread uses few ingredients and is simple to make – even I can bake reasonably edible shortbread!**

꧁ **When all the ingredients are in your mixing bowl (if baking at home you could use your magical cauldron, but make sure it is thoroughly clean), hold your hands over the mixture and repeat this spell three times:**

Sweet as sugar, sweet as candy,
Sweet and warm like cherry brandy,
Stop your sniping, stop your jibes;
Be nice instead – like apple pies!
I work so hard, I try my best,
I don't deserve your evil jests.
Hear now my witch's game;
Be quick to listen, slow to blame.
Taste these good things made for you,
A magical gift from me to you,
A tasty treat of Wiccan power;
So remove the frown, remove the glower.
Only sweet things in my cauldron go,
So you will no more be my foe.
Stop your sniping, stop your jibes;
Crabby teacher, please be nice!

✺ **Continue to bake the biscuits.**

✺ **On the following day, take some into school and offer them to the teacher you've had problems with.**

The magical biscuits should sweeten their temper towards you and lessons should improve.

to help you be more organised

What you want: to get a bit more organisation into your life.
What you need: all your school books and pens etc., your pentacle.
Moon time: full.

- Take all your school things to your altar and arrange them around your pentacle.

- Now hold your hands over the pentacle and concentrate on being completely organised. You always know where your next lesson is and where your books are, you get your homework in on time, ideas for projects come to you easily, you're never late for school and so on.

- Once you have this picture firmly in your mind, say:

  This is who I am ... I am very well
  organised and in complete control.
  So mote it be!

- Now pack away your things neatly and arrange your books, etc. ready for the following day's lessons.

To enhance this spell you might like to colour co-ordinate your pens, pencils, pencil case, etc. And, if your school allows, why not back all your books in trendy paper? Use the magical colour chart on pages 25–6 as your guide.

spells for school and work

bad crowd spell

We have already looked at a couple of balloon spells, so you should know how these work by now. This one is designed to give you the strength to break away from a group of people who you know are not the best to be around. If you are in a seriously bad crowd, then tell a responsible adult whom you trust, as you may need their help.

> **What you want:** to get out of a bad crowd.
> **What you need:** an oak leaf, a balloon of your favourite colour, a pin.
> **Moon time:** waning.

To begin with, hold the oak leaf in your hands and try to absorb the essence of the tree. Do this by visualising a great oak tree swaying in the breeze. You might even see the spirit of the tree peeping out at you from among the branches. To me, the spirit of the oak tree appears as a wizened old wizard; to you, it might appear as something completely different.

Once you have fully envisioned the strength of the oak tree, roll up the leaf and place it inside the balloon through the neck. Now blow up the balloon and tie a knot in the neck.

Once again, use your visualisation skills, this time to magically day-dream what your life will be like when you are free of these people. Tell yourself that you are the strong one and they are weak. You have the strength to stand alone, and even to stand against your former friends if necessary.

Now pop the balloon with the pin and say:

> *As this balloon pops so loud,*
> *I release myself from a bad crowd.*
> *For the free will of all and with harm to none,*
> *My friendship with you is over and done.*

☙ **Remove the oak leaf from the remainder of the balloon and keep it with you as a talisman of strength. You should now find it easier to break off ties with these people and move on with your life.**

To enhance this spell, work it in combination with the Spell for Inner Strength (see pages 39–40), which also calls on the strength of the oak.

black shuck spell

Black Shuck is a phantom dog who has long been associated with what witches call the wild hunt. He is a large black hound (think Hound of the Baskervilles), and you can call on him to protect you on your walks and travels.

> **What you want:** to invoke a hound of protection.
> **What you need:** your imagination.
> **Moon time:** any – use when you need.

☙ **After casting your protection Circle, bring to mind the image of a large black hound. Breathe life into him three times as you have done with your other thought forms (see page 70).**

☙ **Tell him that his purpose is to protect you on your way to school, or wherever you're going. Tell him that he is to meet you at the school gates after your lessons and protect you as you walk home too.**

☙ **Once you are safely home, thank Black Shuck and release him.**

protection spell

This is a basic protection ritual that will help to keep you safe as you go to and from school, or when you are generally out and about. You should always keep your wits about you, your eyes peeled and your ears open. If someone looks dodgy, trust your instincts and avoid them. Remember that magic best helps those who help themselves, so please be sensible and use your common sense whenever you're out. Use this spell every day to help boost your safety shield.

> **What you want:** to be protected on your walk to and from school.
> **What you need:** a tiger's eye crystal, your imagination.
> **Moon time:** any – perform daily.

✧ **Put the tiger's eye on your pentacle and charge it with the powers of protection. Now cast your magic Circle as usual and then say:**

> *This circle is a magical boundary of protection;*
> *It goes where I go, it bends when I bend;*
> *It moves with me and protects me from all things,*
> *Seen and unseen. So mote it be!*

✧ **Snap your fingers to seal the power and know that your Circle will be with you until you release it, which you should do as soon as you have arrived safely home.**

✧ **Take the tiger's eye and keep it with you as a charm. Re-charge it once a month on the full moon.**

Although this ritual may take a little time to begin with, the more you practise, the quicker you will become at casting an effective protection Circle. After a number of years in the Craft, I can now do this in the blink of an eye and with a snap of my fingers, but it has taken me a long time and much practice to get to this stage. Keep practising and use this spell every day, and eventually you too will be able to cast a Circle in a split second.

creativity spell

If you have homework to do or a project to begin, then work this simple spell to assist with your creativity.

> **What you want:** to work creatively in lessons, projects, homework, etc.
> **What you need:** a tea-light or a yellow candle, grapefruit essential oil.
> **Moon time:** full – or use when you need.

✣ **Put a few drops of grapefruit oil on to your tea-light or candle. Grapefruit oil is uplifting and will help you to get energised and begin your work.**

✣ **Place the candle near your work space and light it.**

✣ **Take three deep breaths, sit down at your desk and begin.**

If you need help to work hard in school, simply put a few drops of grapefruit oil on to a tissue or handkerchief and inhale regularly for an instant lift. Keeping your mind uplifted is the first step towards concentration, creativity and hard work. I use this spell whenever I am writing, and it works for me.

revision ritual

What you want: to make your revision effective.

What you need: geranium essential oil, a clear quartz crystal, a tissue, a drink, nibbles, a quiet space to work.

Moon time: full – or use when you need.

🌙 **Sprinkle a few drops of geranium oil on to the tissue and tuck it into your bra or top – the warmth of your body will help the fragrance to waft upwards to your nose.**

🌙 **Take hold of the clear quartz crystal and say:**

> *My mind and my thoughts are as clear as this crystal.*

🌙 **Take everything you need for your revision (including the crystal) to a quiet space and arrange it all neatly.**

🌙 **Also take with you a cold drink such as orange juice and a few nibbles. I usually have a small bowl of sweets on my desk as I write – it helps to make the whole work experience more pleasant!**

Now settle down and begin to revise – write down anything you think you will have trouble remembering. Take regular breaks and keep sipping the juice.

When you need to think something through, eat a sweet, hold the crystal and take a moment. Don't be too hard on yourself – little and often is the key to successful revision.

calming circle for before exams

Exams can be very stressful, and when we are stressed, our performance level is usually affected. Taking a few moments out can help with this. You can do the following exercise alone, but it's better if performed with friends as it will ease the general atmosphere.

> **What you want:** to calm yourself and friends, and put things in perspective.
> **What you need:** your imagination.
> **Moon time:** any – perform five minutes before you go into the exam room.

- **Form a circle with your friends – hold hands or link arms. It is important that the circle is unbroken.**

- **Now close your eyes and imagine that you are standing on the very top of a mountain looking down on a beautiful green valley with a tranquil lake far below.**

- **All your doubts are now in the palm of your hand in the form of shimmering glitter or star dust. Cast the star dust down into the lake, so releasing all doubt, and look around from your vantage point. The world is huge and beautiful, and you can do anything and be anything.**

- **Be positive. If you have worked hard and revised then you should have nothing to worry about. And even if you haven't revised, these exams will just show weaknesses that can be worked on in retakes or at college. And you never know – you may just surprise yourself and get top marks in all your exams.**

job spell

The following type of spell is known to witches as 'petition magic'.

> **What you want:** to find and get the right Saturday job.
> **What you need:** a sheet of paper, a pen.
> **Moon time:** waxing.

✧ **On the sheet of paper, write down all that you want from a Saturday job. Do you only want to work on Saturdays, or are you willing to work on Sundays, after school and during the holidays too? What type of job do you want? A paper round? A job in a clothes or record store? Helping out at a local stable or at a hairdresser's?**

✧ **Fold the paper in half. Now draw a pentagram on both sides of the folded paper and say:**

> *I want this. It is coming to me. So be it.*

✧ **Keep the paper on your altar. When you have found your ideal job, rip up the paper and scatter it to the winds.**

Money Spells

Everyone needs a little financial help now and then, and I have to admit that I'm no stranger to money spells! The important thing to remember with this type of magic is to ask only for as much as you truly need and, as always, to cast your spells with harm to none.

money drawing spell

> **What you want:** to attract money.
> **What you need:** three silver coins (any kind of coin will do), your pentacle, a pen, paper, a magnet.
> **Moon time:** waxing.

- **Take the three silver coins to your altar and place them on your pentacle to form a triangle.**

- **Now on the slip of paper write down the amount of money you need and what you need it for, such as holiday pocket money or a school trip.**

- **Place this paper in the centre of the pentagram so that it is within the triangle of coins. Put the magnet on top.**

- **Leave this spell untouched until the money has arrived. Then put the coins and magnet somewhere safe for future money spells, and burn or bury the spell paper.**

prosperity powder

A magical powder can be scattered along window sills and doorways to attract a magical goal. It can also be used as an incense and burnt on a charcoal block. This prosperity powder is one that I have made and used many times. It smells wonderful and is very powerful.

> **What you want:** to make a scattering powder/incense to encourage prosperity.
> **What you need:** mortar and pestle, empty jar and label, a few drops of patchouli essential oil, 5 ml/1 tsp dried mint, 5 ml/1 tsp basil, 5 ml/1 tsp rosemary, 5 ml/1 tsp cinnamon, 5 ml/1 tsp ground coffee, 1 tea-bag.
> **Moon time:** full.

∴ **First, rip open the tea-bag and empty its contents into the mortar. Add the rest of the dry ingredients and grind to a fine powder.**

∴ **Transfer the powder to the jar and add a few drops of patchouli essential oil. Replace the lid of the jar and shake well. Label the jar 'Prosperity Powder'.**

∴ **Scatter a little of the powder in your purse and money boxes – you can wrap it in tissue first if you like.**

As I get paid through the post, I always scatter a little of this powder inside the letterbox. Use your imagination, but please note that magical powders are not for consumption and should never be ingested.

lucky leaves spell

When you are using this spell, your purse will never be empty.

> **What you want:** to attract money to your purse.
>
> **What you need:** three dried bay leaves, patchouli essential oil, your purse, a paint brush.
>
> **Moon time:** waxing.

∴ Take the leaves and so on to your altar.

∴ Using a paint brush, paint some of the patchouli oil on to each of the leaves. Leave them to dry.

∴ Put the leaves in your purse to draw money magically to you.

to get a debt repaid

> **What you want:** to call in money that is owed to you.
>
> **What you need:** prosperity powder (see page 132), a pen, paper.
>
> **Moon time:** waxing.

∴ On the sheet of paper, write down the full name of the person who owes you money and how much is owed.

∴ Now take a pinch of prosperity powder and scatter it in the middle of the paper saying:

> *The money owed to me and more*
> *Will soon be coming through my door.*

∴ Fold the paper tightly, being careful not to lose any of the powder, then leave it on your magical altar.

∴ When the debt has been paid in full, burn the spell paper, or tear it up and scatter it to the winds.

prosperity tree

A large part of prosperity magic is being grateful for what you already have. This is a spell to help you to feel that.

What you want: to attract good things and give thanks.
What you need: a vase, lots of fallen twigs, luggage labels.
Moon time: full.

∴ **Put the twigs into the vase, arranging them nicely.**

∴ **Now on the luggage labels write down the things that you are grateful for: your computer, for instance, or your mobile phone – I would have killed for my own phone at your age. By acknowledging the prosperity you enjoy already, you will attract more into your life – because like attracts like.**

∴ **Now take one luggage label and on it write something that you really want.**

∴ **Put this label at the foot of the vase and when it has manifested, add it to your tree.**

∴

to make the most of your pocket money

What you want: to be better at organising your money.
What you need: a sheet of paper, a pen, a money box or savings account.
Moon time: waxing.

- On the sheet of paper, write down how much pocket money you get each week.

- Now make a firm decision that you are going to put five to ten per cent into a money box or savings account each week. This will help you to form a positive habit that will be very useful to you in later life. You can save the money for something specific or just for a rainy day.

- Now out of the remainder of your money decide how much you are going to spend on make-up, how much on sweets and chocolate, how much on social events, such as a trip to the cinema with friends, and so on.

- Write all this down on your sheet of paper and then keep it on your altar where you can see it daily. Stick to this spending programme and you will soon have some healthy savings.

to get a raise in pocket money

What you want: to get your pocket money increased.

What you need: paper (to make a boat), a pen, dried mint or prosperity powder (see page 132).

Moon time: waxing.

∴ First make a little boat with the paper. On the side write how much pocket money you would like to get. Be realistic and take into account any financial problems your parents might be having. Try not to be greedy, but put down a sum that you think is reasonable.

∴ Now scatter a little dried mint or prosperity powder into the boat.

∴ Take the boat outside to a lake, pond or stream. Float the boat away to release the magic of your spell.

∴ Wait until the full moon, and on this day tactfully bring up the subject of a possible raise in pocket money. Be prepared to give a little – you may be asked to do small jobs around the house in exchange for extra pocket money. If you agree to this, then you are acting in a very responsible manner, and you can always use the same tactic again further down the line.

to help with savings

What you want: to increase your savings.
What you need: patchouli oil, a black pen, a little notebook.
Moon time: waxing.

- First, write down in the notebook the amount of savings you have. Every time you make a deposit or put coins in your money box, add this sum to your little book. This will soon become a complete record of your finances. And being able to see how your money is accumulating will be a great inspiration to you to keep saving.

- Second, use this old witches' trick on all your money. It is an old magical way to protect your money and bring prosperity into your life.

- Draw a tiny pentagram on all your notes and put a dab of patchouli oil on your coins. This will ensure that any money you spend will come back to you times three.

- Go through your purse every evening, marking any unmarked notes and dabbing oil on to all your coins.

to control your mobile phone bill

What you want: to stop overspending on your mobile phone.
What you need: an old phone bill, black thread, small post-it notes, a pen.
Moon time: waning.

∴ Take the old phone bill and roll it up into a scroll. Secure it with black thread.

∴ On a couple of post-it notes write down the maximum you want your next bill to be. Stick one on the old bill and the other on the back of your phone.

∴ Now whenever you pick up your phone you'll see the note. Ask yourself if the call is really necessary and remember that texting is cheaper.

∴ Keep the old bill by your altar until the new (hopefully lower) bill comes in.

∴ Then throw away the old bill and repeat the spell, perhaps choosing an even lower target and reducing your bill even further.

Heal the World

So far, you have worked spells and magic to improve your life. But that is only half of the Wiccan way. Witches believe that we should also give something back in return for the success of our spells. This completes the exchange of energy and will ensure the continued success of our magic.

One of the ways in which Wiccans give back energy is by performing magic and healing rituals for the Earth. The Earth is our mother and witches are her children, her chosen ones. It is up to us to lead by example and take care of her. Simple things like a household recycling plan or picking up litter can have a huge effect on our world – if more people did them our planet wouldn't be on the brink of global disaster, as it is now.

Witchcraft is the nature-based practice of magic, so it is up to witches at least to make a start in putting right mankind's many wrongs. After all, if we are going to ask the universal energies to help us manifest our deepest wishes and desires, the least we can do is offer a helping hand to our planet when it is in need – as it clearly is.

This chapter is devoted to spells and rituals geared towards Earth healing. Here you will find magical ways to help cleanse the oceans, prevent wars, and protect wildlife. I hope that you will perform at least one of the following spells as a way of giving thanks for all you have and all you enjoy.

to protect the planet

Our planet is under constant attack from various forms of pollution and exploitation 24 hours a day, seven days a week. On the next full moon, perform this simple spell to help ease the pain and stress our world is undergoing.

> **What you want:** to protect the Earth from harmful things.
> **What you need:** a picture of the Earth or a globe, salt, lavender essential oil.
> **Moon time:** full.

- Take the picture or globe and surround it with an unbroken circle of salt. This will create a magical barrier and will help kick-start the world healing process.

- Next, anoint the picture or globe with a few drops of lavender essential oil. Lavender oil is well known for its ability to heal almost anything. Rub the oil into your representation of the Earth using gentle circular motions, as if you were rubbing cream into a burn or wound.

- Once you have anointed the Earth, hold your hands over it and imagine that a stream of healing white light is coming from them and being absorbed by the Earth. You are now giving a little of your energy back to the planet. Continue for a minute or so and then leave your spell set up for a further 24 hours. Your healing magic will then be in progress and you can clear your things away.

to halt or prevent war

What you want: to guard against an outbreak of war or encourage a peaceful solution to conflict.

What you need: an old atlas, a ruler, a pencil, some stickers to represent peace and love (for example, flowers, hearts, rainbows), your pentacle.

Moon time: full.

- Place the stickers on your pentacle to be charged with the powers of love and friendship.

- In the old atlas find the two countries that are at odds with each other. Now draw a line between the two countries, effectively joining them up.

- Next, draw a large pentagram over the two countries and around that draw a love heart that encloses the whole area. Inside the heart stick your stickers and say:

> *With this magic, fight no more.*
> *I cast this spell to stop/prevent the war.*

The spell is now complete, although you may need to repeat it on a monthly basis to reinforce the magic.

peace spell

You will need your artistic skills for this one.

> **What you want:** to encourage world peace.
> **What you need:** a pink envelope, rose petals, felt tip pens or crayons, geranium essential oil.
> **Moon time:** full.

☾ On the back of the pink envelope draw a picture of a dove surrounded by the arc of a beautiful rainbow. Both the dove and the rainbow are traditional symbols of peace. Colour the rainbow and the dove carefully to make a really pretty picture. Now inside the flap of the envelope write your wish for world peace.

☾ Pick up the rose petals and hold them in your hands while you visualise a beautiful, friendly, peaceful world for your generation to inherit.

☾ Once you have a clear picture in your mind, drop the rose petals into the envelope, add three drops of geranium essential oil, seal the envelope and say:

> *So be it.*

☾ Keep the envelope on your altar with the picture facing out into the room.

to cleanse the oceans

The waters of the world are badly polluted. Humans made the mess, so it's up to humans to clean it up. Call on the guardian elementals of water, the mermaids, for this spell. Ask that they take the energy you give and use it to cleanse the oceans, rivers and streams of our planet.

> **What you want:** magically to cleanse the world's oceans, rivers and streams.

What you need: a glass bowl, spring water, blue or green food colouring, a CD of ocean sounds (optional), a mermaid figure (optional).
Moon time: full.

꒳ Fill the bowl with pure spring water and add a drop or two of food colouring to make it look like a beautiful pool of magical water. When I perform this spell I have a CD of ocean waves playing, and I burn sea mist oil in my oil burner. This helps me to connect to the element and the elementals I am trying to assist.

꒳ Sit comfortably with the bowl of water on your knee. Place both hands in the water and gently move them around, feeling the cool softness of the liquid gliding through your fingers.

꒳ Visualise that strong healing white light again, and imagine a tiny, beautiful mermaid swimming up to take this energy from you.

꒳ Close your eyes and think of all the joyful times you have had in the water – days by the river, holidays at the seaside, swimming in the local pool, sinking into a deep bath at the end if a long day. Think of all that water has given you, and give back a little of your energy to the water sprites so that they can go about their job of cleansing the waters of the world.

꒳ At the end of this spell pour the bowl of magical water into a nearby stream or river. Alternatively, you could pour it down the drain, so that it can join up with the oceans later on its journey.

Try to perform this spell at least once a month.

to save wildlife

For this spell you need to be outdoors, either in a park or woodland, or perhaps in your own garden. Wherever you choose, it must have trees.

> **What you want:** to help the wildlife of the world.
> **What you need:** a bottle of bubbles, your imagination.
> **Moon time:** full.

ᔐ **Take your bubbles and sit beneath a tree.**

ᔐ **Next, call upon the Lord of the Greenwood. He is the guardian spirit of all wildlife and lives beneath a canopy of trees. He is known by many names: the Green Man, Herne the Hunter, the Green Knight, the Oak King, the Holly King, Cernnunos, and even Robin Hood. Decide which image of him appeals to you most. I often use Herne the Hunter or Robin Hood, as these were my childhood heroes.**

ᔐ **Bring your chosen image to mind, and when you see him clearly in your mind's eye, begin to think of all the wildlife under his protection.**

ᔐ **Now gently blow bubbles into the forest of trees. Each bubble is filled with your energy, and as it bursts that energy is released. Think of all the animals you are helping to protect with this magical rite – all the rabbits and deer, the foxes and stoats. To begin with, concentrate on the animals that are native to your own country. Then move on in your mind to other animals, perhaps endangered species such as pandas, tigers and whales.**

- ⚷ When you have blown bubbles for around 10–15 minutes, see the Lord of the Greenwood surrounded by a glowing green shimmer. This is the magical energy you have sent him. Watch as he walks away to use your energy where it is needed most.

- ⚷ Put away your bubbles and return home.

to attune with the seasons

The best way to attune with the seasons is to create a nature altar. This is similar to creating a working altar, but your nature altar will change with the seasons.

> **What you want:** to attune yourself with nature through the changing seasons.
> **What you need:** a small table or chest, an altar cloth of a colour appropriate to the season, candles, flowers, plants, rocks, crystals, pebbles, herbs, etc.
> **Moon time:** full.

- ⚷ Cover the table or chest with the altar cloth.

- ⚷ Now decorate your nature altar with seasonal fruits and flowers, natural rocks, crystals and ribbons. Add figures of woodland animals, endangered species or pretty birds. Place on it a candle or two, and maybe a small water feature in the middle. Make your nature altar truly represent the season and change it as the seasons pass.

to communicate with the faeries

The faeries are shy creatures who long ago retreated from our world of war and destruction. They exist just beyond the realm of vision in a region known to witches as the astral plane. However, they do love humans, for all our faults, and if you are patient and open-hearted, you can communicate with them. The following ritual is an ancient wise woman's trick for making contact with the faerie folk.

> **What you want:** to get in touch with the faeries.
> **What you need:** a saucer of milk or honey, a witch's broom.
> **Moon time:** any, but perform on midsummer's eve – 21–22 June.

ᛋ **Decorate the broom with ribbons and bells.**

ᛋ **On midsummer's eve, carry the broom and the saucer of milk or honey out to your garden.**

ᛋ **Prop the broom by the back door – this is a traditional magical invitation to the faeries to enter your life and home.**

ᛋ **Sit quietly for a moment and silently ask the faeries to come to your garden and make merry. Tell them that you wish to be friends. Set down the saucer of milk as a gift to the little people and go indoors.**

If things keep disappearing and getting lost in your home, that is a sure sign of faerie activity! You should also be aware that, according to tradition, faeries can change themselves into hedgehogs in order to walk in our world unnoticed by us. So who knows? You may already have faeries at the bottom of your garden ... you just didn't know it!

earth angel spell

Every planet has its own guardian angel, and this little charm will call on the Earth Angel to assist in world healing and magic. You can use this ritual in addition to any of the other spells in this chapter.

> **What you want:** to invoke the angel of the Earth.
> **What you need:** an open mind and heart, a statue of an angel.
> **Moon time:** full.

᛬ **Call on the Earth Angel with this invocation:**

> *Earth Angel, I call you here,*
> *To make the oceans bright and clear,*
> *Make the forests grow strong and true,*
> *Bring abundance for all – make hardships few,*
> *Strip the air of poison and harm,*
> *Where war is threatened, bring peace and calm,*
> *Guard all animals and protect them with love,*
> *Light up the world with stars from above,*
> *Embrace the world and make it well,*
> *Heal our planet and heed this spell.*
> *So mote it be!*

The Wheel of the Year

In addition to spell-castings and magic, witches hold special celebrations throughout the year to welcome the changing seasons. These celebrations are traditionally known as sabbats. There are eight sabbats in all, which together make up the Wheel of the Year. Sabbats are a time for celebration, fun, music and dance. They are also good times to set goals for the future while acknowledging how far we have come along our path and giving thanks for all the lessons life has taught us so far.

Often witches will gather together in groups for the celebrations, although sabbats can also be celebrated by a witch alone. I prefer to hold my celebrations by myself, as whenever I have attempted to bring a group of friends together, usually around Halloween, something unexpected has always come up, leaving me with a minor mountain of food to dispose of! You may have more luck in your preparations with like-minded friends, or, like me, you may prefer to keep the sabbats alone. I am a solitary witch after all. So celebrate the sabbats however you like, with friends or without; it's up to you. But do make sure that you acknowledge each sabbat in some way, as the sabbats are at the very core of the Craft.

Samhain – 31 October

We begin with Samhain (pronounced sow-een), as this is the witches' new year. Traditionally called Halloween by non-witches, it was the last day of the old Celtic calendar and is perhaps our most important sabbat – which is probably why it is a night when witches are believed to jump on broomsticks and fly. I wish!

Samhain is a harvest festival, so decorate your nature altar with apples, grains and berries. Add an orange altar cloth, a couple of black candles and a pumpkin, and you're up and running.

The sabbat of Samhain is generally a time of reflection. We release past hurts and anything that is no longer any good to us, and we begin to look ahead. Samhain is the perfect time for divination and fortune-telling, so get out your pendulum or buy some glass beads and make your own rune stones. Your ritual should also include a quiet time for you to think of all you have achieved over the past 12 months. Then enjoy yourself – light candles, eat Halloween foods, watch a spooky film such as *The Craft* and read or tell ghost stories.

Enjoy the sabbat and embrace the season. That's what witchcraft is all about.

Yule – 21–22 *December*

Yule is the time of the winter solstice – the shortest day and the longest night, with more than 12 hours of darkness. There has been a celebration feast in mid-winter for centuries because it helps to brighten up the dark days of winter and gives us something to look forward to.

Yule is probably my favourite time of year, when the trees are decorated, presents are wrapped and there are parties to go to. It is a time of coming together with family and friends. Many of today's Christmas traditions actually date back to early pagan festivals and the old religion of witchcraft.

The time of the winter solstice is very magical and there is a strange stillness to the Earth, as if nature itself is calmly waiting for the spring and the rebirth of the sun. Of course, in most homes Yule is simply a part of the run-up to Christmas, but to witches Yule is the main festival, while the Christian Christmas takes a back seat.

To decorate your altar for Yuletide cover it with a dark green cloth and arrange sprigs of holly around it. Ivy and mistletoe are also traditional altar decorations at this time of year, as are little silver bells, which are associated with Herne the Hunter and Mother Earth. Your candles should be red and green, and you might like to burn a winter incense such as pine or cinnamon. To celebrate this sabbat, make your own cards and give them to friends. Buy little presents, as gift giving is another Yuletide tradition.

Your ritual should be personal to you, as should all your rituals, but you might like to listen to carols or go carol singing with your friends – 'The Holly and the Ivy' is actually an ancient pagan song. Traditional foods are roast chestnuts, joints of meat, and spiced fruit pies and puddings.

Celebrate by watching a seasonal film such as *A Christmas Carol* (I read this Dickens classic every year in December) or *Holiday Inn. The Lion, the Witch and the Wardrobe* also illustrates the spirit of the season.

You might like to buy a fat red candle and light it for Yule. Or if your house has an open fireplace, you could burn a genuine Yule log that you have found on a woodland walk.

Celebrate in any way that suits you and your family.

Imbolc – 2 February

The world outside is cold, wet and frozen. It's time to rush home from school to a warm house and a hot drink, and curl up in a nook with a good book and the family cat.

Although the weather is still cold and miserable, the sabbat of Imbolc is a sign that winter is almost over and spring will soon be here. It is a time when the roots of plants are first stirring deep down in the earth and the sap within the trees is slowly beginning to rise. In the past, it was the time when the first lambs were born.

Decorate your altar with any early flowers you can find, with candles and with ribbons of pale pinks and greens. Burn sandlewood or lavender incense. Another traditional altar decoration for this sabbat is the corn dolly, which can be bought from most florists' and craft shops.

Traditional foods include rice pudding, milk and home-baked bread. The festival of Imbolc begins the cycle of spring cleaning, and you should use this time of year to clear out your room, getting rid of anything you don't need or use. You could also include a cleansing and purification rite as part of your ritual. Protection magic for the home is often reinforced on this sabbat, helping to create a space of love and peace for the family. Your ritual should conclude with a magical bath, to which you have added essential oils or herbs of your choice.

Another tradition is to light up the home with candles, as Imbolc is also known as the Festival of Lights.

Ostara – 21–22 March

Ostara is known in the Christian calendar as Easter, and, as with Yuletide and Christmas, there are many similarities between the two traditions. Ostara takes place on the spring equinox, when night and day are of equal length. The date varies slightly from year to year, but it is on or around 21 March.

Ostara is truly the beginning of spring – a time of awakenings and a quickening within the earth and the animal kingdom. It is a time of planting and new life, when the trees and other vegetation renew themselves for another cycle of life.

At this sabbat a witch's altar is generally decorated with daffodils and other spring flowers. The altar cloth is usually of a lovely springtime colour or a floral design. Figures of rabbits and hares, chicks and lambs all have a place on a springtime altar. And, as this is a time of new life, eggs (preferably chocolate ones!) are also seen in abundance.

Floral incenses such as violet and honeysuckle are burnt at this sabbat. Flowers and eggs are given as gifts. We cast spells for prosperity during the coming months, and celebrate the season by reading about and communicating with the faerie folk, who make the Earth grow green after its long winter sleep.

Make your ritual a joyful celebration of new life. If you can, visit the countryside and see the baby animals in the fields. Plant bulbs in the garden, decorate hard-boiled eggs, buy flowers for someone you love. Try writing a faerie story and finish your ritual with a movie such as *Fairy Tale, A True Story*.

Beltane – 30 April

Beltane is the fertility sabbat – and that doesn't just mean babies and children! At Beltane witches cast spells for the fertility and growth of projects and business ventures, and general spells for success. We also work towards the protection and continued fertility and abundance of the Earth. Beltane is also known as Walpurgis Night, which means 'the night of the witches'. It is a powerful time when the world has been awakened into life, and animals are finding mates and performing their own rituals!

Beltane is a good time for faerie magic – though most seasons of life and growth are a great time for working with the little folk. The Queen of the May is actually a symbolic representation of the Faerie Queen. Traditionally, bonfires, known as the Beltane fires, are lit at this sabbat, and we welcome the growth of light and the lengthening of days.

To celebrate Beltane, decorate your altar with red and white, the traditional colours of this sabbat. Light red and white candles, go for walks in the woods (Sherwood is beautiful at any time of year and is always magical), or take part in local May Day celebrations and festivals, such as parades and the May Pole.

Add a picture or figure of a stag to your Beltane altar. The stag represents Herne the Hunter, and witches honour him at this time. This is also the time of Robin Hood, so dig out books and films and re-live the old tales.

Traditional foods are grapes, strawberries and other fruits, with fruit juices to drink. This is also a good time to go looking for a fallen twig to use as your wand or to make daisy chains and flower wreaths to decorate your altar. Make your ritual a celebration of the lengthening days and give thanks for all the good food our world gives to us.

Litha – 21–22 June

Litha, also known as midsummer's day or the summer solstice, is the time when the sun is at its peak. This is the longest day; from now on the days will gradually shorten, bringing in the darker nights of autumn and winter.

Litha is a time of great celebration, when many people choose to go off to sacred sites such as Stonehenge and hold their rites there – the Druids are famous for this. Midsummer is also a good time for handfastings, the witches' wedding ceremony. Traditionally this is the sabbat for the strongest workings of faerie magic – when you may even feel or see these wonderful beings!

Your altar should be covered with a yellow or gold altar cloth, gold candles and sun-shaped ornaments. You might like to burn an incense made up of dried mint, basil, lavender and thyme. Another tradition at this sabbat is to tie pretty ribbons to a tree while making a wish – the tree spirit will grant your wish in due course.

Traditional foods for the Litha sabbat include honey, fruit and ice cream. This is also a good time to make personal protection charms. Make your Litha ritual represent who you are and your lifestyle. Give thanks for any summer holidays you are planning on taking, and enjoy the sabbat and all that the season of summer has to offer.

Lughnasadh – 1 August

Lughnasadh (pronounced Loo-nas-ah) is the ancient Celtic festival dedicated to the god of fire, Lugh. At this time of year it is still warm, but there is the first tang of autumn on the breeze. This sabbat is the festival of the grain and signals the approach of the waning year, with the prospect of autumn and winter just around the corner.

Lughnasadh is also a time of cleansing and, once again, a cleansing and purification rite should be part of your ritual. To decorate your altar for this sabbat use the colours of the harvest: gold, deep yellow, russet and maybe a touch of bronze. Put out plates of sunflower seeds and nuts, and add a little basket of blackberries to your altar too.

Lughnasadh is the corn festival, and it is traditional to bake bread for this sabbat. This bread should be shaped into the form of a man to represent John Barleycorn, the god of the harvest who is cut down each year, only to return with another crop the following summer.

If baking bread isn't your thing (as it isn't mine) then do what I do: take a baguette and inscribe a matchstick man on to the top using a kitchen knife. Then fill the bread with your favourite sandwich filling. Next, cut the head clean off to symbolise the corn god's sacrifice, and put this out as a gift to the birds and wildlife. Enjoy the remainder of the baguette as part of your ritual feast, along with blackcurrant juice and apple and blackberry pie.

Mabon – 21–22 September

Mabon is the autumnal equinox – once again day and night are of equal length. From now on the days will become visibly shorter and the nights darker. I have to admit that winter is my favourite time of year, and I love all the winter sabbats. I look forward to the long dark nights and the first touch of frost or snow biting in the air. I find the natural fragrance of winter truly invigorating.

Mabon is named after the Welsh god of harvest and is traditionally a time of thanksgiving. The colours of the harvest and the first fallen leaves should decorate your altar, along with pine cones and acorns. This is a very relaxed sabbat, at which witches step back and acknowledge all that the harvest of their lives has brought them – this could be a new job, great exam results, a valuable lesson learned, a first driving lesson and so on.

Burning bayberry, either as incense or in the form of a scented candle, is said to bring money throughout the next 12 months.

Traditional foods are stews, hot pies and corn on the cob, with hot chocolate to drink.

This ritual should be a time for you to give thanks for all the good things in your life, to release the bad and to look forward to the future.

Samhain – 31 October

The Wheel has turned one full cycle and we have moved forwards in our lives by a year. I hope that you enjoy all the sabbats and create your own rituals to fit into your life and make a statement – not only about who you are but also about who you truly want to be.

Afterword

Well, that's it. I hope you have enjoyed this little book of spells. If you would like to learn more about magic and spell-casting, read my book *Candleburning Rituals*, which has in-depth information about the concept of magic and has even more nifty spells for you to try!

Always remember that to be a witch means to take control of your destiny – you can be whoever and whatever you want to be. All you have to do is focus, try hard and cast the spells.

I have truly enjoyed creating this little book for you, the witches of tomorrow. Feel free to write to me via my publishers and let me know how you liked *Everyday Spells for a Teenage Witch*, but please enclose a stamped addressed envelope if you would like a reply.

Finally, I hope that your life is all that you want it to be and all that you can make it ... may all your dreams come true!

Take care, my magical reader, until our next merry meeting. Blessed be!

Morgana

Index